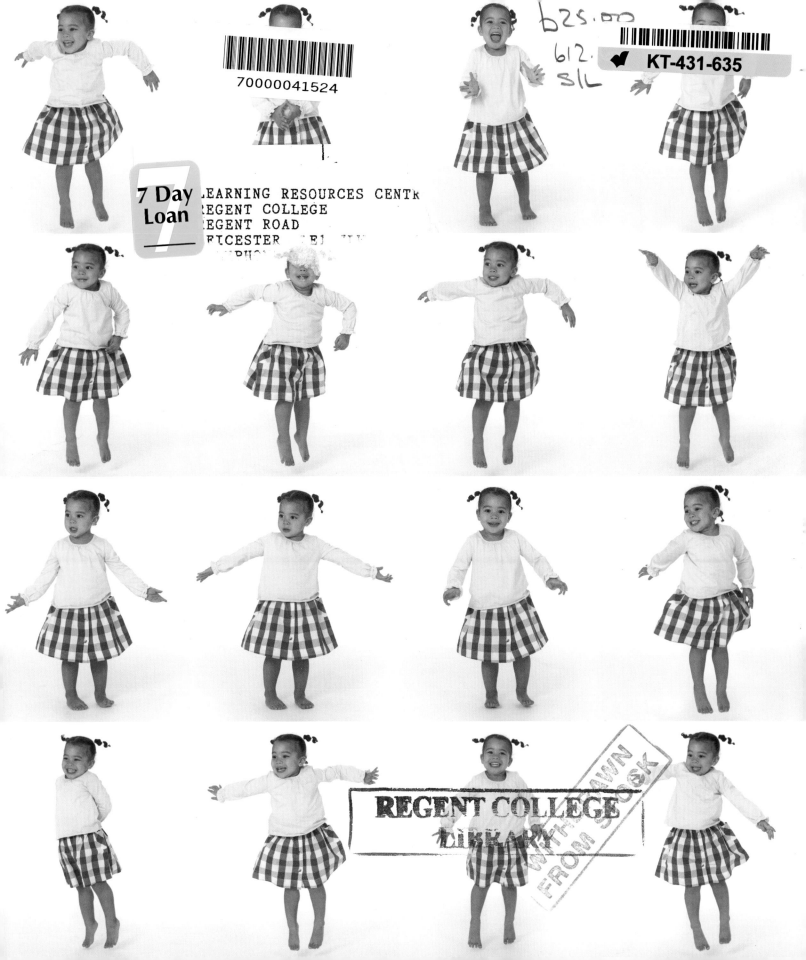

child

child

how children think, learn and grow in the early years

desmond morris

hamlyn

An Hachette UK Company
www.hachette.co.uk

First published in Great Britain in 2010 by
Hamlyn, a division of Octopus Publishing Group Ltd
Endeavour House
189 Shaftesbury Avenue
London
WC2H 8JY
www.octopusbooks.co.uk

Distributed in the U.S. and Canada by Octopus Books USA:
c/o Hachette Book Group
237 Park Avenue
New York, NY 10017

ISBN 978-0-600-61994-9

A CIP catalogue record for this book is available from the
British Library.

Printed and bound in China

10 9 8 7 6 5 4 3 2 1

Note
This book is not intended as a substitute for personal
medical advice. The reader should consult a physician in all
matters relating to health and particularly in respect of any
symptoms that may require diagnosis or medical attention.
While the advice and information are believed to be
accurate and true at the time of going to press, neither the
author nor the publisher can accept any legal responsibility
or liability for errors or omissions that may be made.

contents

foreword

For a loving parent, the years of a child aged from 2 to 5 are often some of the most delightful. The heavy demands of caring for the human baby are past and now, at last, it is possible to communicate verbally. The pre-school child, able to walk, talk, run and explore, has his entire life before him and the whole of the planet to investigate. The joys of watching him learning to understand his own body and his physical capabilities are immense. His energy is boundless and his curiosity endless. Every day is full of new discoveries, new adventures and new activities. It is a magical time for both child and parent.

From babyhood to school time

This book provides a portrait of what it is like to be a human child between the ages of 2 and 5. It is a sequel to *Baby* – the amazing story of the first two years of life. Together these two volumes cover the whole period before the first day at school, when the small child starts to become regimented into the learning system of his culture. For the next ten years or more, he will become educated into the ways of thinking of the society in which he lives – his time divided between parents and teachers. But before that happens there is a brief period of just a few years when the active child is closest to his parents. They have the best opportunity, not only to relish the special moments of play and childhood discovery, and to witness the unfolding of a unique new human personality, but also to impart their personal values to their offspring. The details of the lessons learnt by the child during this phase may be forgotten in later years, but their impact is lasting.

Socially interactive

In tribal societies, it is very rare for mothers to be separated from their little ones during this early phase of childhood; when they are at work their children are always nearby. In our modern, urban societies this is not always possible. Some mothers are able to stay at home during the whole of this period and experience every moment of the pre-school child's development, but others go to work, leaving their young ones in the care of dedicated child minders. For some mothers this is a sacrifice they would prefer not to make, but there is much to be said for nursery schools and similar environments, in that they prevent young children becoming isolated from others of their own age. Tribal children mix freely together, and this early socializing has always been a part of the human story since its earliest days. It is only the modern trend of living in houses separated from one another by locked doors, walls and fences that has given rise to the isolation of the pre-school child. So the nursery school is more natural to human society than one might imagine. It takes the place of the open space at the centre of the early tribal settlement, where everyone mixes together and social encounters are frequent and varied.

Freedom versus risk

The biggest problem for the pre-school child is how to explore his exciting new environment without taking undue risks. The child that is treated with an excess of caution may well miss out on many of the most entertaining aspects of growing up. The child that is allowed to run wild may enjoy days full of rich experiences, but is so unaware of dangers and hazards, that he can easily get into serious difficulties. The lucky child is the one who is provided with safe environments in which he has as much freedom as possible. Time taken to allow a child to explore his body movements freely, and to experience the thrills of running and jumping on safe surfaces is well rewarded.

stepping stones

the developing child

The pre-school period is one in which huge changes take place. The body becomes stronger and develops improved physical control. There is boundless energy and an intense curiosity about the environment in which a child finds himself. His brain continues to mature, allowing new ways of experiencing the world and of thinking more clearly about the exciting challenges it has to offer. Above all, the small vocabulary of the 2-year-old, expressed in an inarticulate way, blossoms at an amazing speed into a wonderfully advanced, grammatically organized, verbal communication system by the time the child reaches the age of 5 and is about to start school.

Every child is different

Although all children go through similar phases of development between the ages of 2 and 5, it must never be forgotten that every child is unique. Some are slow to make the expected advances as the months pass; others are faster than usual. These differences usually mean very little. Slow starters catch up later on, while fast learners eventually slow down a little. Some individuals are slow in one respect, say physical growth, but fast in others, say mental progress. Unless one of these differences becomes severe they can safely be ignored. Only if they become extreme is it necessary to seek professional advice.

The study of children

Learning the truth about the way in which very young children develop is not easy. It requires immense patience and the ability to make objective observations that are free from personal prejudice. In the past, some of the greatest experts in child development based their ideas largely on what they observed in the behaviour of their own children. A natural love for their own offspring could lead to their results being biased. Others have avoided this pitfall, and yet their sample has been too small, or too local. Before we can make any general statements with confidence, we have to be sure that they apply to children in more than one culture and that they are based on a large enough sample.

Simple experiments

Many interesting results have been obtained by carrying out very simple experiments with small children. For example, children are asked to play a game with marbles in which they can win some pennies. Each game player is told that there is another child who has no pennies at all, and that it would be kind to put one in a bowl for him. With some children the adult who tells them this then puts one of her own pennies in the bowl and leaves. With other children the adult explains again, but leaves without putting a penny in the bowl. It has been found that children are less likely to be generous if the adult does not set a good example. From this it can be predicted that, in other cases, learning by example will probably be more effective than learning by instruction.

Such tests may seem obvious, but for child psychologists it is important to be sure that 'common sense' is scientifically valid. Every so often, a 'well-known fact' turns out to be a fallacy and it is important to run these fallacies to ground.

An important feature of the marbles experiment is that it is fun for the children. Some earlier psychological experiments sometimes involved tests that caused stress. Today, great care is taken to avoid all such testing.

Direct observations

Some students of child behaviour prefer not to carry out any experiments at all, but choose simply to watch what children do in playgroups or elsewhere. These observers keep copious notes and record how the frequency of certain actions increases or decreases as circumstances change. In this way, simply by watching, they can arrive at very precise and detailed conclusions concerning such things as the social interactions of children and the changes these undergo as the months pass.

nature versus nurture

For many years there has been a fierce debate between those who believe that the human child is a blank slate on which anything can be written, and those who argue that the child comes in to the world equipped with a set of inborn, genetically controlled behaviour patterns. The truth, we now know, lies somewhere between these two extremes.

Genes versus family influences

In recent years, evidence of the genetic control of human behaviour has been growing, thanks to new techniques that enable scientists to examine the structure of DNA. It is clear that many of the ways in which children develop in their early years occur without any outside influences. For example, a child that is born blind smiles when she is happy. Such a child has no idea what a smile looks like – her disability robs her of any chance of learning how to smile from clues in her environment – yet the reaction occurs at an appropriate moment nevertheless. Smiling is, therefore, basically an inborn response, a part of human nature, not a part of human nurture.

However, if you look at the smile of the blind child it is not like those of other children. The mouth is certainly smiling, but, unable to see other smiles, the blind child cannot refine its action. In other words, the basic smiling action may be inborn, but it requires visual feedback to perfect it.

Environmental influences

This combination of genetic influence, modified and improved through learning and experience, is what happens with most of the actions and reactions of young children. It is as if they have inherited, not a set of rigid genetic rules, but rather a collection of inborn suggestions that then become moulded by the environment. We are all programmed to talk, and the basic structure of language is the same the world over, with words and sentences, nouns and verbs, past tense and future tense, grammar and syntax, but we all develop a personal style of talking and speak in many different languages. Our genes make us babble and give us the motivation to organize that early babbling into an elaborate form of verbal communication, but the precise details of our verbalizations are too complex to be left to the genes. These details must come from social feedback, from learning from our parents, our siblings, our friends and our teachers.

The importance of early learning

Early learning does more than simply refine behavioural reactions, however. It is now known that the way in which we are exposed to various environmental experiences may also influence the growth of the brain. The human brain is designed with a degree of plasticity. If it is stimulated in certain ways during very early childhood, this can alter its structure. For example, as the brain develops, there is an ongoing process of wiring and rewiring the brain cells. New connections, or synapses, are constantly being formed, while others are lost. The brain is programmed to produce a huge number of these connections when the child is very young – as many as a thousand trillion. This is more than the brain needs later on in life, but it is as if the genes that programme the early development of the brain are saying 'here you are, use what you want of these'. Then, as time goes by, the principle of 'use it or lose it' comes into play. Connections that are used are kept, while those that are not used are pruned away. This increases the efficiency of the brain by removing 'dead wood' and retaining only those nerve connections that have a role to play.

It follows from this that a pre-school child who is forced to live in a sterile or deprived environment, starved of brain stimulation, will not simply become ignorant but will also suffer from an over-pruning of the synapses in the brain. This causes long-term disadvantages, so it is vitally important for a small child to be exposed to a wide variety of experiences. Her young brain will be laying down the foundations that make it easier to respond to such experiences in a sophisticated way at a later age.

the rich environment

The benefits to a child of playful parents with a strong sense of curiosity and a zest for living are tremendous. Parents who provide a richly varied and stimulating environment for their growing child also give him the very best chance of becoming a talented, intelligent adult. Between the ages of 2 and 5, the human brain is like blotting paper, absorbing huge amounts of information from the world around. If the childhood environment is boringly monotonous this cannot happen.

A world of music

It has often been said 'show me a musical child and I will show you musical parents.' Many young children are given music lessons, but it seems to be those whose parents are musical themselves who are most likely to develop an early talent in this field. This reveals an interesting feature of child learning. Witnessing adult enjoyment at a particular kind of activity appears to have a greater impact than being given formal teaching. If the child sees that his parents or other role models derive great pleasure from an activity, this acts as a powerful stimulus to do likewise. A house that is always full of music, for example, makes music an important pursuit in the small child's mind. The best-known example of this is Mozart, who grew up in an intensely musical family and who was, himself, composing at the age of 5.

Language and classification

Children between the ages of 2 and 5 are capable of absorbing astonishing amounts of verbal information. If they happen to be fortunate enough to grow up in a multilingual environment, they quickly learn more than one tongue. And the sooner they are exposed to such experiences the easier it is for them to become increasingly multilingual later in life.

It is astonishing how advanced a small child can become, given a suitably stimulating environment. American, William James Sidis, could read and write at the age of 2; Charles Bennet of Manchester could speak in several languages at the age of 3; and the British philosopher, John Stuart Mill, could read Greek at the age of 3. Such examples reveal that the brain of the pre-school child is all too often underestimated.

Parents who make a game out of collecting information, soon develop a passion for identification and classification in their children. For example, a 4-year-old boy travels regularly with his father, who makes a game of identifying the brand of other cars that pass them on the road. Before long, the boy is able to identify over 100 makes of car. This particular ability may have no serious application in the adult world, and yet it activates and enriches that part of the brain which is concerned in general with the classification of objects in the environment. As an adult, that particular boy will therefore have a brain that is capable of ordering information with increased efficiency.

Encouragement by example

Some children are pushed by their parents into taking a greater interest in a particular activity. The parents are then disappointed when the child fails to become engaged. This is because a young child is more stimulated by activities in which the adult displays a genuine interest. His brain is very sensitive to what you find exciting and fun to do, and is remarkably good at spotting (and ignoring) faked enthusiasm.

personality traits

As soon as they reach the age of 2, children start to show a particular type of personality. Most common at this age is a temperament that is active, outgoing, self-centred and full of curiosity. Between the ages of 2 and 5, this basic pattern becomes modified in a number of ways, depending on the innate nature of the child and the environmental obstacles she encounters.

Active or passive?

Although most pre-school children are extroverts who are intensely active some are, by nature, rather more passive. This passivity is more difficult to interpret than high levels of activity because it may be the result of several different types of personality development.

A child who finds it difficult to interact with the outside world, may perhaps be suffering from a mild form of autism. Or it may reflect the fact that a child has become increasingly introverted, with a great deal going on inside her brain, but with no desire to externalize her thoughts. When he was a very young child, the famous author Aldous Huxley was seen to be sitting silently gazing out of a window. When his nanny asked him what he was thinking about, he replied 'skin'. Clearly, complex thoughts were taking place inside his head, but he was not driven to share them with others.

In complete contrast, some children develop a passive temperament because there really is very little going on inside their heads. Still others are quiet because they are shy when in company. A shy child has a personality that is active and bold in familiar surroundings, but quiet and withdrawn in unfamiliar settings. Finally, there is the serene child, who is by nature quiet. She is deceptively passive because, in her quiet way, she may be as active as any noisy child – she just doesn't make so much fuss.

Dominant or submissive?

Some young children are, by nature, rather confident and sure of themselves, even in strange company. A child whose parents have heaped praise on her to a point where she feels tremendously important, may expect similar treatment from strangers. With adults she shows an unusual degree of confidence; with other children she seeks a dominant role and expects them to submit to her will. Such a child may go on to become an obnoxious bully or one of the world's great leaders, or perhaps both.

Parents who give in to a child's every whim, may create a child who is assertively overconfident and who will find the first days at school a sharp learning curve, when she loses parental support and has to stand alone for the first time.

The child who is warmly praised for her strong points and her achievements and is mildly criticized for her weak points and her failures, is more likely to achieve a healthy balance between dominance and submissiveness in her dealings with others. She takes a dominant role where it is appropriate, but she does not expect it as her right.

Brave or cautious?

Some children lack any form of caution, throwing themselves into every activity, no matter how dangerous. Others show excessive caution when faced with a novel or risky situation. Achieving a happy balance is not always easy. Extreme lack of caution may be praised as bravery or condemned as wild stupidity. Extreme caution may be viewed as common sense or as cowardice. This ambivalence can be confusing to a small child.

Personality pros and cons

There are many other personality 'opposites', such as volatile or easy-going, practical or romantic, analytical or intuitive and kind or self-centred. An individual with a well-balanced childhood will manage to achieve a happy medium in most of the cases. For some, a more extreme personality type may prove to be a curse, while for others it becomes the basis of their greatest adult achievements.

gender differences

It is sometimes said that boys and girls are only different in their behaviour because they are treated differently by adults and have adult stereotypes imposed upon them. It is argued that if, as small children, boys and girls are treated in exactly the same way, they will develop the same sort of personalities and interests, and gender differences will disappear. New research on the human brain has proved conclusively that this is not true. From the day they are born, the brains of boys and girls show striking differences, primarily in the way in which they function.

Early development

Inside the womb, the foetus is subjected to the release of hormones that influence the way in which the brain develops. The result is that, even at this very early stage, male and female brains start to show differences in the way they operate. Because these differences are not visible to the naked eye, it has been possible for some commentators to claim that they do not exist. Differences in sexual anatomy between boys and girls are so obvious that they are beyond doubt, but differences in personality have lacked this advantage. As a result there has been a long-running battle between those who believe that masculine and feminine behaviour is a myth perpetrated by adults who give toy swords to little boys and sewing kits to little girls, and those who believe that there are inborn differences between the sexes.

Problem solving

Fortunately, we now have new research tools that make it possible, once and for all, to assess the similarities and differences in the brains of young boys and young girls. During the past three decades, special equipment has been designed that enables us to check the way in which the human brain works, without involving any surgical procedure. Simply by placing a subject inside a large machine, it is possible to watch changes in the activity of the brain as it deals with different tasks. When this is done, it immediately becomes clear that male and female brains operate differently when dealing with the same problem.

The most valuable new tool for studying brain activity is a device that produces magnetic resonance images. The electrical activity of the brain is recorded as the subject deals with different tasks, and then magnetic fields and radio waves are used to create high-quality images. These images show us which parts of the brain become active when particular problems are being solved. If a subject is asked, for example, to solve a verbal teaser or a mathematical puzzle, it is possible to see different parts of the brain lighting up, while other parts remain quiet. When the recordings are complete, it is then possible to compare male brains with female brains to see how many differences appear.

Verbal and spatial tasks

When boys and girls are given a verbal task, such as deciding whether two words rhyme with one another, brain scans reveal that in a boy's brain the left hemisphere is much more active than the right. In a girl's brain, during identical tests, both hemispheres are active. This means that boys and girls actually think differently about verbal tasks and solve them in different ways. It also means that the male brain is more specialized than that of the female, using one part of the brain for one task and another part for something else. The female brain, by contrast, often uses both sides of the brain to solve problems.

Another difference in male and female brains is that males have a right hemisphere that is slightly larger than the left. In girls the two hemispheres are more or less the same size. One result of this is that boys have an advantage when it comes to dealing with spatial problems (such as the mental rotation of objects in space), because these are solved in the right hemisphere.

the only child

Being an only child has both advantages and disadvantages. The only child has the full attention of her parents and grandparents, yet this can be a mixed blessing. She may get more personal attention and more intense loving care, but parental expectations are also higher, and she is under greater pressure to succeed. This may cause undue stress and an over-conscientious personality.

The disadvantages

In earlier times, when larger families were the norm, the only child might have been looked upon as an unfortunate oddity, pampered and fussed over by her doting parents. Not only did the parents have more time to devote to her, but they were also more concerned about her safety because, if she died, they were left completely childless. Their whole parental investment was wrapped up in her and, as a result, she was treated differently from a child with siblings.

The outcome of this, it was believed, was that the only child became more self-centred, more full of herself and more determined to get her own way than a child with siblings. At the same time, she might be subjected to such high expectations that she could develop anxieties connected to an exaggerated need to succeed. Having no brothers or sisters with whom to rub shoulders in everyday life, she might also become increasingly poor at socializing and joining in with groups.

The advantages

Recent studies have shown that these older ideas are often unfounded and that the advantages of being an only child frequently outweigh the disadvantages. Having an enriched environment – one that does not have to be shared with others – leads to better intellectual development. The only child is, on average, slightly more intelligent than a sibling.

The only child is also, on average, a higher achiever. Her parents expect it of her and she struggles to please them. Like all 'driven' individuals, she may be more prone to anxiety if she fails and lacks the sunny, easy-going, take-it-or-leave-it attitudes of members of a big family, but that is a price that all high achievers have to pay.

The only child may find socializing more difficult, but when she does join a group, she is more likely to show leadership qualities. Also, although the only child, on average, has fewer friends, she does have the same number of very close friends. In other words, she may lack the need for a highly active social life, but is just as capable of forging close bonds of attachment with a few special companions.

Making the most of it

If the only child is brighter and a better achiever, how can one avoid the other side of the coin, namely being self-centred and unsociable? Clearly the great intelligence and motivation of the only child comes from greater parental attention and encouragement, but is it easy for them to provide these benefits without creating what has been called 'a little emperor'? The answer lies in ensuring that she does not become too solitary, but from an early age is thrust into playgroups where she will find that she is not always the centre of attention. Siblings learn this every day at home, but she is starved of the rough-and-tumble of group activities and needs more of these. Given both the full attention of her parents at home and the socializing effect of playgroups away from home, the only child can have the best of both worlds, being a high achiever who is nevertheless a cheerfully sociable being.

How common are only children today?

In the West, the number of families with only one child has been showing a gradual increase and today the figure stands at about one in five. The reason for the increase is that people are leaving it later to have children and couples tend not to stay together as much as they used to. In addition, more women are going out to work and these factors all contribute to the favouring of smaller families.

birth order

Parents with large families are well aware that, from birth, their children may show marked differences in personality, even though they are treated in the same way and grow up in the same environment. Some of these changes owe much to genetic variations, but others are the result of birth order – whether the child is the first-born, the second, or the third, and so on. Adapting to the arrival of a sibling does affect each child's personality.

The first-born child

In some respects the first-born child has a personality that is similar to that of the only child. This is because, for a while at least, until the second child appears, he *is* the only child in the family. Typically, he is hard working, spends longer at school, and is more adult-oriented. He also needs more adult approval than later-born children. He is less carefree, more zealous and shows greater perseverance. Compared with later children, he is also self-reliant, independent, undemonstrative and sometimes rather shy. As his young life unfolds he is seen to dispense with the carefree pleasures of childhood more rapidly than his later siblings, to become more serious and responsible, and to try and transform himself into a 'little adult'.

One big difference between the first-born and the only child is that, as he grows up, the first-born does not spend a great deal of time at home alone. The only child becomes adapted to being on his own for long periods of time and may even come to enjoy solitude. Loneliness is not something that the first-born has to conquer.

For the first-born, the moment when the second child arrives can be difficult. If it is handled badly by the parents who, as they fuss over the new baby start ignoring their first child, the transition can be a painful one. It takes a conscious effort on the part of sensitive parents to divert their attention occasionally from the new baby and to demonstrate clearly their surviving love of the first-born. This is not easy, because the new baby is so novel and so demanding, but it is crucially important if the first-born is not to feel discouraged and disillusioned. Involving him with caring and playing with the new baby, and making some time just for him, will help during this transition.

The second-born child

The second child is tougher, more easy-going and more insensitive to adult scolding than the first child. He tends to be a pleasure-seeker, who reacts strongly to the wonder and beauty of life. In some cases he may also show a stubborn, rebellious streak that the first child usually lacks.

As he grows older, the second child may sometimes try to compete with, and overtake, the first-born in various ways. If the first-born's higher status proves hard to challenge, this discovery may often lead to second-child naughtiness. If he finds he cannot compete, he will start to rebel. If, on the other hand, he is less competitive, he may leave serious matters to his first-born sibling and instead focus more on fun and games. He will, in the process, become less practical and more romantic, more of a dreamer than one who is concerned with worldly matters

The third child

The third child has been described as the 'odd one out', who is rather restrained and self-conscious and sometimes difficult to get on with, but who may compensate for this by becoming something of a visionary.

The special problem that the third child has to face is that his two older siblings have developed a bond between them before he even existed. He arrives in the world to find them attached to one another and with himself on the outside, looking in. Early on, he discovers that he is excluded from some activities because he is 'too young' and is left to sulk or scream while the two elder siblings go off together. He can react to this situation in one of two ways – a circumstance that keeps on repeating itself. He can try his hardest to join the older siblings and share their senior status, or he can give up and build an emotional wall around himself, inside which he creates his own personal goals. His major problem is to avoid a feeling of inferiority, of being neglected or rejected. If, despite his efforts to belong, he eventually comes to see himself as an outsider, he may grow up to become more distrustful of other people than is the case with his siblings.

The fourth child

The fourth child is typically most like the first one, repeating his qualities. The fifth is like the second and the sixth is like the third, and so on.

family variations

There are so many variations in the age structure of human families, that predictions about the personalities of the only child, the first-born, the second-born and the third-born must always be viewed as trends or slight biases, rather than as fixed rules. When large numbers of children are studied, the differences are valid, but there are always going to be individual children who do not fit the general pattern. This is because family circumstances – from age gaps to social environment – differ so much.

The age gap

For example, a first-born child who has to wait for five years before the arrival of a sibling is going to be more like an only child in personality than one whose sibling arrives quickly after only one year. Having reached the age of 5 as the sole child in the family home, the first-born will already have built up the personality type of an only child before the influences of a younger sibling begin to make their mark. Whenever there is a long delay between the arrival of siblings, the personality differences between the children will not necessarily be typical of their 'birth order' position.

Neighbourly contact

Architecture also plays an important role in influencing the 'birth order' personalities. For example, the only child of a family living in an enclave where the children of close neighbours all mix freely together, is going to be less solitary than a child growing up in a detached house with no close neighbours. Urban children tend to be more isolated from one another than suburban children, and suburban children more isolated than village children. Children living in small tribes, where the family units all mix together, are the least isolated of all and 'birth order' differences are at their weakest. Also, poor children living in slums or ghettos are more exposed to social mixing than rich children living in mansions or on big estates.

These, and other outside factors, influence the development of personalities and create variations of the general rules of 'birth order'. But despite this, it is certainly true that, for most families, the personality differences of the first, second, third and later children, described here, strike a chord and go part of the way to explaining the diverse personality differences they observe inside the family home.

twins and triplets

When twins or triplets are born, the rules of 'birth order' receive another challenge. Which of the twins will become the senior child? Will there be endless arguments between them? Fortunately, one twin is always born some minutes before the other and parents always seem to record this difference, and refer to one twin as the 'elder', even if the time difference is only a few minutes.

Amusingly, twins themselves always mention this whenever the subject of sibling seniority is raised. Although the time difference is trivial, the need for a sibling 'pecking order' is so great that 20 minutes, say, is treated as though it is 20 months, and, on this basis, the relationship between the twins becomes artificially normalized.

Over a period of years, being a twin creates a complex attitude towards the companion. Because of their unusual degree of similarity, the two become very close to one another, as if they are two elements of a single individual. This is especially true of identical twins. On the other hand, because there is no conspicuous physical or mental seniority of the type seen between siblings with several years between them, there is a heightened competitiveness. These two features of being a twin – increased oneness and increased antagonism – often create a complicated ambivalent relationship of a type that the ordinary, single-birth sibling never has to face.

Twin studies

Until recently the study of twins who were separated as babies was widely used as a means of ascertaining the influences on development: heritability (variation explained by genetic differences), shared environment (those aspects of environment that are common to all siblings), and non-shared environment (aspects of environment that may be different within a family as a result of birth order, schools attended, the way children are treated differently by their parents, and so on). These days, as mentioned previously, advances in techniques of gene analysis make scientists less reliant on these studies and help towards the ongoing nature-nurture debate where twins, both identical and non-identical, make fascinating subjects.

the physical journey

the growing body

When a child reaches the age of 2, his growth rate decreases significantly. The rapid increases seen in infancy are no longer recorded. There is, from this point onwards, an increase in height of about 6.5–9 cm (2½–3½ in) a year. Annual increases in weight vary from 1–2.75 kg (2–6 lb).

However, although increases in overall height and weight may be less dramatic, between the ages of 2 and 5 a child's body undergoes a progressive change in proportion. There is also a steady improvement in coordination and movement skills. This growth is stimulated by growth hormones released by the pituitary gland, however environmental and hereditary triggers are also believed to be influential in development.

A sleeker body

With each year there is considerable change in the child's shape, his arms and legs growing proportionally longer in relation to the rest of his body. It is as if the head and trunk are more advanced in growth than the limbs during infancy. Then, at 2 years, the limbs start to stretch out and catch up, achieving a better balance with the head and torso – at the age of 3, a child's head is approximately one-sixth of his body size; by the age of 5, this figure is closer to one-seventh. At the same time, the rounded curves of the baby give way to a more angular shape. Lean muscle replaces body fat, and the toddler's protruding tummy disappears. The straighter frame becomes much stronger, in line with an increasingly active lifestyle. As the child progresses from 2 to 5 years old, the lower part of his face increases proportionally in size, as the teeth and jaws develop.

Bladder and bowel control

Almost every child develops the ability to stay dry between the ages of 2 and 5. By the age of 5 most children have developed full bladder control, both by day and by night. By day, the problem is usually brought under control very early, between the ages of 2 and 3. Night-time control progresses more slowly: at the age of 5, some 15 per cent of all children still wet the bed occasionally. Bowel control usually arrives by the age of 4 and soiling is rare after that.

The active child

This is an age at which the growing child needs to express himself daily with a great deal of physical exercise, followed by plenty of sleep at night. His diet needs to be balanced and varied to fuel this activity and to continue his growth.

One of the dangers facing the pre-school child today is that there is not enough safe, open space for him to express his urge for vigorous physical activity. The urban child, all too often, is encouraged to reduce his natural physical exuberance and this can be problematic. It has been estimated that, in advanced countries, 14 per cent of today's pre-school children are obese. Thirty years ago the figure was only 5 per cent. This owes much to the prevalence of the television as a means of entertainment. This does not mean that there should be a ban on television for young children, only that it should not be allowed to interfere with energetic physical activities and that it only occurs in a period of rest.

Fortunately, children are amazingly resilient and can quickly shed extra pounds and improve physical fitness, given the right environment. For some, this will not happen until they find themselves enjoying the sports and gymnastics of schooldays.

Typical growth rates

Although there are variations from child to child, there are average heights and weights for children between the ages of 2 and 5 (see pages 58–59 and 110–111). Interestingly, height varies less than weight. This is because skeletal growth is more stable than the amount of body fat that is being laid down by different eating and exercise habits.

gross motor skills

During a child's exciting journey between the ages of 2 and 5, her body becomes much stronger and her muscles better developed. At the same time her skeletal system and nervous system matures, giving her a more advanced control over her muscular actions. As a result there are progressive improvements in both the gross motor skills and the fine motor skills (see pages 34–35). The gross motor skills are those involving actions of the whole body, such as walking, running, sitting, climbing and various athletic movements, and seem to develop slightly faster in boys than girls, giving them the edge on outdoor activities.

Muscle power

One of the great joys of being a 4- or 5-year-old child is the discovery of the thrill of vigorous muscular activity. Every day brings a new physical experience, a novel way of leaping, jumping, running or climbing. It is as if the straightjacket that kept the helpless baby condemned to immobility has been removed, releasing all the pent-up energy that was just waiting to express itself. Children will find ways of exploring this new physicality at home or in the freedom of the playground or open spaces.

To see a pre-school child run loose on a beach is to observe nothing less than the sheer joy of living. A tiny athlete has emerged from her cocoon and is flinging herself about with wild abandon. As the informal play patterns unfold, they reveal the way in which the child spontaneously invents a new theme and then starts to vary it. This 'thematic variation' is the very basis of creative thinking. Here it is handled at the primitive level of whole-body movement and action. Later in life, it becomes the basis of human innovation in pursuits as diverse as art and science.

The child playing on the beach tries out new types of locomotion – running, leaping and skipping along – then dramatically throws herself to the ground, rolls over and tests the soft surface with her hands. She runs back and forth avoiding the waves, chases after a ball, digs in the sand and makes marks on its wet surface with a stick.

The remarkable feature of all these activities is that there is no need for parental encouragement or instruction. There is an internal energy and a powerful motivation, not only to be physically intensely active, but also to vary these activities as much as possible. Primary play patterns are not imposed, they are spontaneous. Secondary play patterns are greedily added to the primary ones. These do involve at least some degree of parental direction, in the form of simple games with basic rules, such as throwing a ball or kicking it at a goal, or playing chasing games.

Physical skills

Between the ages of 2 and 5, the child learns to master many basic physical skills, such as climbing and descending the stairs or a ladder, balancing on one foot and holding that position for a while, jumping or hopping on the spot, throwing a ball, catching thrown objects, hopping on one foot, skipping with a rope, and spinning round and round like a whirling dervish.

The following list of actions are among those that adults might encourage, one way or another, by playing with the child during this phase of childhood:

balancing, bending, bouncing, catching, climbing, crawling, dancing, galloping, hanging, hauling, hitting, hopping, jumping, kicking, leaping, lifting, prancing, pulling, pushing, riding, rolling, running, skipping, sliding, stepping, stretching, swaying, swinging, twisting, turning, throwing, tumbling and walking.

This list may not be complete, but it already shows the amazing versatility of the human body and the exciting range of movements and actions that are available to the pre-school child. Many of these actions can be encouraged in the playground and pre-school gymnastic classes are the perfect place to help build confidence and abilities.

fine motor skills

The fine motor skills are those that involve the more subtle actions of the hands, wrists, fingers, feet, toes, lips and tongue. Like the gross motor skills (see pages 32–33), these show considerable improvement in the pre-school years, the coordination between hand and eye becoming increasingly refined and the dexterity and strength of the fingers, in particular, becoming greatly advanced. Girls tend to master fine motor skills sooner than boys, giving them an 'indoor advantage' as opposed to the boys' 'outdoor advantage'.

Dextrous fingers

The human hand has two grips: the power grip and the precision grip. The power grip involves grasping an object by curling all four fingers around it and then curling the thumb around the opposite side. In this grip the four fingers work as one. By contrast, in the precision grip, the fingers work to differing degrees. The typical precision grip involves only the thumb and forefinger, brought together in opposition to pick up, hold or move a small object. Some actions require a modification of this precision grip, using more than one finger against the thumb.

Writing, drawing and precision painting, for example, see the thumb placed in opposition to the first two fingers. But the very young child sometimes tries to hold the pencil or brush between the thumb and all four fingers, and only refines this action as he grows older.

Using scissors shows several variants. It may start out as a thumb and forefinger action. It may then improve to a thumb and second finger action, with the first finger acting as a support digit. (See also, Using Scissors, pages 62–63.)

A delicate twisting, turning or rotating action may use all five digits, but, unlike the power grip, only employs the tips of the four fingers and the thumb.

In general, the pre-school child gradually improves his finger holding actions by reducing the number of fingers employed. This can also be seen in non-holding actions, such as pointing. The very small baby indicates a direction using all five digits. Only later, at around 18 months, does he refine this to give the adult version of pointing, with just the forefinger extended. The action of pressing a button becomes refined in the same way. While late development in pointing may be insignificant, the inability to do this has been linked to autism so checking for this forms part of a range of tests used to detect the condition.

Improved manipulation

For the toddler, the hand is an organ that slaps, touches and grasps, but as the years pass it becomes increasingly employed as a refined manipulating device. It is this dexterity that has been a vital part in our evolutionary success story, giving us the chance to learn complex manual skills and develop intricate technologies.

The hands of the tiny child start out clumsily, but soon show remarkable improvements in the accuracy of his actions. Some of these improvements are the result of 'hands-on' adult teaching, some the result of simply watching what adults do and then copying it, and some the result of trial-and-error, with the child himself finding a more sophisticated version of a primitive grasp or hold.

For these improvements to occur, the pre-school child must repeatedly be put in a situation where manual dexterity is an asset. Some toys require more delicate handling than others, and if these are regularly made available they will stimulate manual experimentation that will lead to finger refinements of the kind mentioned above. Activities such as drawing, painting, modelling, cutting, stringing beads, pouring liquids and puzzle-solving all help to improve manual coordination. Watching children grappling earnestly with these problems, it is clear that these are much more than mere trivia.

left- or right-handed

By the time children attend school, each one is either left-handed or right-handed. As with adults, 10 per cent are left-handed and 90 per cent are right-handed. Among pre-school children, however, this bias is not so clear, and a child may confuse her parents by being left-handed one day and right-handed the next.

Early ambiguity

During his first few months, a baby gives no clear indication as to whether he will be left-handed or right-handed when he grows up. Then, as time passes, he shows a preference for the left, then the right, then the left again, and back and forth in a long series of pendulum swings. At the age of 2 years, the right hand is usually the dominant one, but by 2¼ confusion returns, with neither hand dominating. This condition lasts for about a year, until the child is 3¼. At this point a gradual preference develops for one hand or the other and, by 4 years, this preference is more or less fixed for the rest of the child's life.

Much has been written about the special personality of the left-hander, picturing him as a rebel, eccentric or underdog. In some cultures there is a powerful effort to prevent a child from becoming left-handed, with naturally left-handed individuals being forced to use the right hand, much against their will. The truth is that, despite folk tales and popular wisdom, there is very little difference, overall, in the personalities of left-handers and right-handers.

Body biases

In ordinary speech, we always refer to a lateral bias as being either left-handed or right-handed, but the hands are not the only part of the body to show such a bias. All chilrden are, for example, also left-eyed or right-eyed, and this can be revealed when asking a child to use a telescope, which he instinctively raises to his dominant eye. The same is true if he looks down a microscope, peers through a camera, or uses any other similar equipment. Surprisingly, most people do not know whether they are left-eyed or right-eyed, but every time they look at something, one eye will be working slightly harder than the other.

It is often said that a professional footballer has a 'good left foot' or a 'strong right foot', or that he took the ball on his 'favourite foot'. This is a foot-bias that he will have first shown when he was about 4 or 5 years old, and which has been with him ever since. When a pre-school child plays at kicking a ball it is easy to spot which of his feet is the dominant one, as he will use this more frequently, especially with his first kick of the day.

Each child also develops a bias in which one thumb is dominant over the other. Notice how he brings his hands together and interlocks his fingers. When he does this you will find that one thumb, the dominant one, is placed on top of the other.

There are many other ways in which one side of the body is favoured over the other. Does the child always use one particular hand to throw a ball, for example? If listening to a distant sound does he turn his head slightly, so that the left, or perhaps right, ear is given preference?

If individual children have all their different lateral biases checked, it is rare to find one child in which everything is on the left or everything is on the right. There is nearly always an overall lateral bias but, at the same time, some parts of the body work the other way.

eating habits

Human beings evolved as omnivores and fare best on a varied diet. One of the problems with the pre-school child is that she often develops favourite foods and is resistant to trying out new tastes, especially ones with strong flavours.

It is important to remember that, not so long ago, when she was a baby at the breast, the child's diet was anything but varied, consisting of a single sweet substance. As a result, sweet tastes are still strongly favoured by the 2- to 5-year-old, and this is perfectly natural. The big difference now, however, is that the pre-school child is increasingly active, with boundless energy, and this expenditure of energy demands a diet that provides a much wider range of essential nutrients.

Forcing new foods on to a child may create strongly negative reactions that become difficult to eliminate when she is older. The best practice, therefore, is to proceed slowly but surely; she will get there in the end. One technique that seems to work is placing small amounts of a new food alongside an old, favourite one. If the child is suspicious of the new food, she can then take her own time to try it out.

Little and often

A child's stomach equates roughly to the size of her fist. Ideally, therefore, between the ages of 2 and 5, the pre-school child needs a number of small meals each day rather than a few big ones. This is not always convenient, but the problem is best solved by interspersing main meals with several snack meals. Parents occasionally worry because their small children do not eat very much at the main meals, but the stomach can tell when it is full and each child knows its own needs. Adults must adjust to the idea of diet by snacking rather than diet by feasting.

A healthy balance

Recommended calorie intake for the 13.5 kg (30 lb) child varies from 700 to 1,700 calories a day, but there is little point sticking to a fixed calorie count, because a toddler may eat a large amount one day and very little the next. It makes more sense to focus on the quality and variety of the child's diet. The small child needs a daily intake of carbohydrates, proteins, vitamins and minerals. Energy-rich carbohydrates, along with fibre and some vitamins and minerals, can be obtained from bread, cereal, fruits and vegetables. Proteins and other vitamins and minerals, especially iron and zinc, can be obtained from meats. And protein and calcium can be gained from various dairy products.

Those adults who enjoy a restricted diet – vegetarians, fruitarians and vegans, for example – should resist introducing the same diet to a very young child. Such restricted diets are not appropriate for the rapidly growing body of the pre-school child. Instead, she flourishes best if given the widely varied, omnivorous diet with which our species successfully evolved. For example, only meat can provide the eight amino acids in the correct balance that a growing human body needs as part of her healthy diet.

health and wellbeing

A child frequently suffers from some kind of minor ailment between the ages of 2 and 5. This is the time of life when immunity to various pathogens is being gained, with the child's system gradually becoming more resistant. Although this is a useful process in general, there is always the risk that one of the ailments might turn out to be something more than a passing nuisance, and it is necessary to be on the alert for this.

Coughs and colds

It may seem that the pre-school child is forever catching a cold. Even a normally healthy child may come down with as many as five to eight colds a year. By the time he has started school, however, he will have acquired antibodies that will protect him, reducing the incidence of colds to an average of only two or three a year. The reason the colds do not disappear altogether is that there are over 200 different kinds of cold virus and it is almost impossible to develop immunity to all of them.

Records show that pre-school children who attend playgroups suffer from more colds than those that are looked after at home. The reason is obvious enough: at the care centre there is more mixing and, therefore, greater exposure to infection. The problem with cold viruses is that they are able to survive for several hours on the hands of children, which means that any games involving hand-to-hand contact quickly spread a cold infection around an entire playgroup.

Early protection

Babies are given standard immunizations during the first few months of life and the pre-school child is routinely given booster shots at the age of 3 or 4. Vaccinations against diptheria, tetanus, whooping cough and polio (one injection), and measles, mumps and rubella (second injection) are the ones usually offered. These pre-school boosters help the child to develop a powerful resistance to these diseases, should they be encountered during schooldays later on. Other, non-routine immunizations, such as the BCG vaccination against tuberculosis, are also offered in areas where there is a higher risk of coming into contact with the virus.

Keeping clean

Some children seem to enjoy messy games and deliberately getting dirty, while others are naturally fastidious and keep themselves excessively clean. As far as health is concerned, both extremes have their dangers. The child who likes getting dirty is more likely to pick up viruses, while the child who is squeaky clean is more likely to succumb to viruses on the rare occasions that he is exposed to them. A happy medium, giving natural immunities without undue risks, is the ideal solution for a healthy child.

With global tourism and family holidays abroad becoming increasingly common, it is important for the child to be given a little extra protection in foreign lands. Some of the most appealingly exotic locations are found in countries where serious diseases may still lurk. If these are absent at home, a small child will be vulnerable and hygiene precautions are more essential.

Keeping safe

When he is very young, a child's body has weaknesses that not all adults appreciate. For example, his field of vision is smaller than that of an adult, and he finds it harder to see things clearly out of the corners of his eyes. As a result he is unable to use information that comes to him from peripheral vision. This puts him at a distinct disadvantage in a busy traffic situation, for example. The approaching vehicle may seem obvious to the adult, but the small child simply doesn't spot it until it is too late.

A young child is also poor at detecting the direction of warning sounds. As a result, he may move towards danger rather than away from it. He also has the courage of the innocent; he has no idea about the dangers of a car that is going very fast and feels no vulnerability in places where a little helpful fear would go a long way to saving him. He has illogical ideas about proportion, believing that a large car moves more quickly than a small car, or that narrow streets are less dangerous than wider ones. Without much experience, he makes up his own rules and these often prove to be based on something irrelevant, taken from another context. He may be bad at judging the speed at which other people or objects are moving and makes poor calculations based on these mistaken ideas.

If more than one thing is happening at a time, a child may not be able to focus on several elements at once. In an emergency, therefore, a complex chain of events may be too much for him. He can also be distracted easily, at times when strict concentration is needed. He may act more on impulse rather than work things out carefully, and he is not always good at staying still at times when movement may be hazardous.

Because adults look after him most of the time, a child tends to think that all adults are there to help him. In road situations he believes that, if he can see a driver coming towards him, the driver must also be able to see him just as well. Finally, his small stature means that he cannot always see clearly what is happening around him.

sleep

In an ideal world, a toddler falls asleep easily at the same time each night, sleeps right through until morning without interruption, and then awakens fully refreshed and ready to face the new day. Sadly, not all pre-school children are able to follow this nightly pattern and many of them have problems getting off to sleep, or find that they wake up during the night. What are the reasons for these variations?

How much sleep?

Like adults, small children vary in the amount of sleep that they require each night. A very rough guide is 13 hours for the 2-year-old, 12 for the 3-year-old, 11 for the 4-year-old and 10 for the 5-year-old. However, there is enormous individual variation, and providing the child has a regular, peacefully uninterrupted night-time sleep, it does not matter if he sleeps an hour or two more or less.

On average, today's children are getting less sleep than recommended by experts. This is worrying, as a failure to get off to sleep and disturbed sleep can affect a child's neurological development, possibly leading to learning and behavioural problems, such as hyperactivity. Children who get a better night's sleep tend to have longer attention spans, are more sociable and make fewer demands.

What kind of sleep?

The kind of sleep a child enjoys changes gradually as she grows older. A baby spends as much as half her slumbers in REM (rapid eye movement) sleep. Between the ages of 2 and 5, the amount of REM sleep, relative to the total time spent asleep, gradually decreases from around 25 per cent to 20 per cent. What is interesting, is that REM sleep is the time when we are dreaming, so it would seem that the younger we are the more we need to dream.

Afternoon naps

Between the ages of 2 and 5, children gradually stop sleeping during the day. As with so many childhood patterns, there is considerable variation, and it is easier to allow the child to take the lead. As daytime napping starts to disappear many parents provide a 'quiet time' during the afternoon when the child can relax.

Nightmares

Roughly 20 per cent of children aged 5 suffer nightmares, but happily there appear to be no long-term consequences. One of the main causes seems to be witnessing a violent incident. A child will be left with a memory of something truly terrible that she does not know how to handle. In her dreams, her confusion returns and she revisits a moment of frightening violence that wakes her up.

Another cause is a secret misery, such as being bullied by an older sibling, that a child takes to bed with her and cannot share with her protectors. If she fears being bullied again tomorrow, but does not tell anyone, this experience may also resurface in bad dreams in some disguised form.

A child that wakes up during a nightmare is usually able to describe it. The next day she may even be able to make a drawing of it. From these descriptions it may be possible to detect the cause of the problem and deal with it.

Night terrors

Night terrors are more dramatic and alarming than nightmares, but fortunately they are far less common and most children soon outgrow them. During a night terror a child appears to be awake, but in reality is still fast asleep and has only partially woken from a deep, non-REM phase of sleep, usually in the first hour after falling asleep. Her eyes are open and she stares ahead, sweating and talking or shouting to herself, and unaware of a protector arriving in the bedroom. Cuddling and comforting simply do not work here. All a parent can do is to switch on the light and make sure that the child does not hurt herself or leave her room. Night terrors only last a few minutes and are not remembered by the child in the morning.

freedom of movement

There is considerable development in locomotion during the pre-school years. This is the result of three important physical changes between the ages of 2 and 5 years. The first is the development of much stronger musculature, the second is the better coordination of limb movements and the third is a more refined sense of balance. These three advances help to turn the still rather clumsy 2-year-old into a lively, athletic 5-year-old.

Early walking

Almost every child learns to walk between the ages of 1 and 2. As a toddler, he keeps his legs rather wide apart and usually hesitates between each step he takes, the body jerking from side to side with each forward step, and the arms held out in front as if anticipating a fall.

By the time he has reached the age of 2, he then enters a year in which this clumsy toddler gait gradually improves. He keeps his feet closer together, and his arms are now more likely to be down by his sides. The walking action is less flat-footed and more like the smooth heel-to-toe action of an adult. As the year progresses he starts to try out short bouts of running and also experiments with jumping up and down. Balancing on one foot, however, requires great concentration.

Because locomotion is such a new activity for the 2-year-old, he is liable to make many mistakes, leading to trips, falls and spills. When this happens there are usually tears of frustration and a great deal of carer sympathy is needed. The ideal world for an active 2-year-old is one with a soft landing – on thick carpet, grass or sand.

Walking with confidence

After a year of practice, the 3-year-old is at last a competent and confident walker. Finding himself excitingly nimble on his feet, he takes great pleasure in tasks that entail active walking, running and jumping. He relishes the extra muscle power that he finds coming from his legs and, in play, will often enjoy stopping and starting suddenly, or swinging sharply to the left or right. This freedom of movement makes for a wonderful new pastime and he makes the most of it. However, although he finds walking and running increasingly easy and effortless, he may still have trouble with some leg actions, such as standing on tiptoe. These may continue to cause him difficulties and require a special effort of concentration.

Children aged 3 show a gradual improvement in their balancing abilities and they no longer watch their steps as they take them. In a special test, half of all 3-year-olds were able to walk a distance of up to 3 m (10 ft) on a 2.5-cm (1-in) wide white line without deviating from it. The 3-year-old is also capable of walking heel-to-toe for a distance of up to 3 m (10 ft) and, with a great effort of concentration, balance with one foot raised off the ground for up to four seconds. He can also broad jump – that is, he can leap forward from a standing start, covering a distance of up to 25 cm (10 in). He can hop one-footed for up to three steps, but without much precision or rhythm.

Walking with precision

At the age of 4, a child can follow a circular path marked out on the floor, without deviating from it. Hopping on one foot, she can manage up to six steps.

From walking to running

At 5, the pre-school child is able to stand on one foot with her arms folded for up to five seconds. Running becomes more streamlined, with the arms performing the smoothly alternating, reciprocal actions of the kind used by adults.

Running also becomes much faster, with the 5-year-old capable of covering 3.5 m (12 ft) in a second.

When the 5-year-old is about to come to the end of the pre-school period, she is capable of rhythmically hopping on the spot, switching from one foot to the other and, during the ever-popular game of hopscotch, leaping accurately into the large squares chalked on the paving stones. Hopping forward on one foot, she can manage up to ten steps and can broad jump up to 90 cm (3 ft). The act of skipping, however, is still primitive at this age and usually involves skipping on one foot while walking on the other.

clambering and climbing

Almost every pre-school child loves to climb. He is not so good at descending, but going upwards is always a thrill. The earliest signs of the passion for this activity appear when a toddler tries to heave himself up onto a sofa or an armchair – an activity that is swiftly followed by crawling up stairs. Once walking has been conquered, there is the excitement of walking up stairs, first with a handhold and both feet placed on each step, then, later, without hand support and with alternating steps. Finally, there is the more difficult descent.

Some child authorities place great importance on daily climbing routines for pre-school children. They argue that climbing is a complex activity that promotes healthy brain development, muscular strength, nervous system development, limb coordination, and balancing skills.

One of the most enjoyable forms of early play-climbing is clambering to the top of a slope, standing up on top of it and then jumping off on to a soft surface below. This will be

repeated time after time. At a slightly more advanced stage, playgrounds often have low-climbing structures suitable for the pre-school child, where he can enjoy taking small risks under careful adult supervision. In the country, small trees or fallen logs provide great challenges, although at the beginning there is usually a demand by the child that the parent or carer stays very close by in case the climber gets stuck and cannot move forward or descend backward.

Playground slides solve the problem of descending. The small child clambers bravely up the steps leading to the top of the slide and then avoids the unpleasantly awkward experience of having to climb back down again, by shooting down the slide. Again, this activity will be repeated time after time, showing just how challenging and rewarding it is for a tiny child to conquer a height.

ball play

A child's skill at throwing and catching develops a great deal between the ages of 2 and 5. A small child will probably learn to throw an object by himself without much training, because throwing is such a primeval action of the human species, dating back to our earliest days as hunter-gatherers. Catching is more difficult for the very young and this benefits considerably from adult teaching.

The allure of throwing

The act of throwing comes as a great discovery to the toddler in a highchair at mealtimes. The action starts out as dropping rather than throwing and is accidental, but the child notices that adults become very excited when food is splattered all over the kitchen. He also notices that these adults are very keen to play a game called 'clean up the mess', so he does his best to join in. Now, instead of just dropping something, he actively flings it away from his body, making an even bigger mess and causing an even more vigorous reaction. This is fun and the toddler has now stepped onto the first rung of the long ladder that will eventually see him thrilling a crowd as a baseball pitcher, a bowler, a darts champion or an Olympic discus thrower.

The first step after the messy food-throwing stage is ball-throwing, and the 2-year-old is capable of learning that some things may be thrown, while others may not. A good supply of foam balls helps in this training, as the child gradually learns how to arch the arm backwards, fling it forwards and open the hand at just the right moment to release the ball to maximum effect. A child will learn first how to throw accurately underarm before mastering the technique of the overarm throw. Throwing at a target, such as a large bucket, helps to improve the aiming element. Once this has been done, the next problem is to prevent things being thrown directly at people. If a child throws a ball at a little friend and hits her, an angry overreaction on the part of the parent or carer registers as a success to the small child. In the child's brain it means that, if he hits someone with a thrown object, the result is a great deal of adult attention. So he does it again. He only finds this hitting action unpleasant if it results in the cessation of the game altogether for a short while.

The challenge of catching

Catching is much more difficult for a small child to accomplish. Unlike throwing, the action has no primeval precedent, and requires a more precise hand-eye coordination. It is an action that nearly always requires patient parental training, with countless failures and then a few successes and, finally, regular success and a feeling of triumph on the part of the tiny catcher. At first, the child only catches balls thrown straight at the chest; he misses those thrown to the side. Gradually this extra skill is acquired and ball games become more and more rewarding.

As time passes, the pre-school child learns to improve his catching skills little by little, catching smaller balls rather than large ones, and catching them in his cupped hands instead of by hugging them to his body. Eventually he may even reach out and manage a one-handed catch, like an adult, after which he is set for the serious games of his schooldays and will also enjoy the challenge of playing with flying discs and similar toys.

riding a bike

One of the great thrills for the small child is that of owning her first set of wheels. The sudden increase in mobility that this offers, and the joy of successfully operating a serious piece of machinery, has a powerful appeal.

Four wheels to two wheels

For many children, the first experience of wheels comes in a push-car or pedal car. Toddlers soon master how to propel themselves along on pushalong vehicles and at around 3 years old learn to use pedals with the arrival of the tricycle – popular because it has a proper saddle and handlebars, and the feel of being on a bicycle without any of the balancing problems. By 4 years old the child is usually an expert at moving backwards, forwards, and starting and stopping with ease. The next stage is the bicycle itself, with added training wheels. These two very small wheels help to avoid a loss of balance. This is the hardest part as he gets to grips with a two-wheeler. Not only is he higher off the ground, there is a whole new issue of balance and braking to test his concentration, coordination and confidence. The small child now appears to be even closer to a true cyclist, but again without the fear of falling over. Then comes the moment of truth, when a parent removes the training wheels and the child takes off on a proper bicycle for the very first time. It takes a certain amount of determination and bravado to cope with the inevitable spills and wobbles, but persistence brings a huge reward and the grown-up feeling of entering the world of adult transportation.

The age of the bike-rider

There has been much debate over the correct age for teaching a child to ride a bike. One view is that, as soon as there is a serious interest in the subject, teaching should begin. An opposing view says that a child should wait until at least the age of 5 before even considering this activity. What are the facts?

A poll taken of 3,000 children revealed that 7 per cent of them had already achieved the stage of unaided bicycle riding by the age of 3; 14 per cent had their first proper ride at 4; and 22 per cent at 5. This means that nearly half of all children were capable of riding a bike during the pre-school phase. So it would seem that this curious human skill, which looks so easy and yet involves a truly complex and advanced form of body balancing, is possible even at a remarkably tender age. However, as with any new skill, parents should never attempt to force a child to do something before they are physically or mentally ready.

Late starters

A number of children find this task unusually difficult, and no fewer than 7 per cent of children only manage their first ride at the age of 8, while 4 per cent are as old as 9 before they can cycle efficiently. Careful observations reveal that the main difficulty is the need to master balance and propulsion at the same time. Rotating the pedals forward with the feet is an action that interferes with simple body balance and it is this conflict that some children seem to find hard to master. The way to overcome this is by making sure that a child's saddle is low enough for her to be able to touch the ground with both feet at the same time. Then, on gently sloping ground she can let the bike move forward until she feels balanced enough to take her feet off the ground. If she starts to wobble she can quickly touch down again. Once she has taught herself to balance as she moves forward, she can then add the additional act of pedalling.

the child gymnast

Almost every pre-school child loves to express himself physically with simple gymnastic activities. Because of his tender age this should always be supervised by an adult, as the more daring child may not yet be aware of the dangers of falling and hurting himself when he engages in the more exaggerated and difficult movements. Pre-school gymnastics should be simple and fun, rather than aiming at some kind of perfect performance.

Trampoline

Bouncing on a trampoline is an ideal form of exercise for the 2- to 5-year-old child. The magnified reward that he receives as the spring of the trampoline surface shoots him into the air provides an immediate physical pleasure. Variety can be introduced gradually, starting with the 'seat drop' and then the 'hands and knees drop'. Later, at about the age of 4, other actions such as the 'back drop' can be added. Trampolining uses up a great deal of surplus energy and at the same time gives the child a chance to 'frighten himself safely' and in this way to experience 'fear management', allowing him to test his physical potential.

Tumbling and rolling

Tumbling, somersaults, cartwheels, forward rolling (from the age of 2), backward rolling (usually attempted at a later age than the forward roll), sideways 'log rolling', handstands and headstands are all actions that create physical challenges for pre-school children. Carried out on a soft surface where falling over causes no harm, and with adult assistance, performing these gymnastic actions can help a great deal to teach the child about the limits and muscular abilities of his body.

It has recently been suggested that 'toddler tumbling' and other gymnastics for the very young will help to build their bodies to develop stronger muscles. According to one specialist doctor there is, in fact, no evidence that simple pre-school gymnastics helps in body-building or improved muscular development, but he sees nothing wrong in these early activities provided the children find them fun and are not pushed beyond their limit.

motor-planning

At about the age of 4, a child develops the ability to perform tasks that involve what is called 'motor-planning'. This entails a particular sequence of movements that lead to an end goal. Each movement on its own may not cause a problem, but the difficulty begins when different actions have to be combined to produce a result, as in threading or tying up a shoelace.

Threading laces

Many types of shoe come with complicated laces that have to be threaded through holes and then the laces tied up. Performing these actions successfully is not an easy task for the pre-school child and requires patient teaching by an adult. A child responds more quickly if the task is slowly and carefully demonstrated by an adult, and if each unit in a chain of actions is taken separately and conquered one by one. A task of this kind requires good hand-eye coordination, the application of concentration that lasts until the task is completed, and the ability to make two hands work together.

Before attempting the difficult task of lacing a shoe or tying a shoelace a child needs to master a simple threading action. Objects such as big beads or cotton reels with a large central hole can be threaded together to form a simple necklace. In this way the single action of threading a cord through a hole can become familiar. On achieving this, the child can progress to the next step, which is to make the holes smaller and to use a shoelace as the thread.

After completing this stage successfully, it is possible to move on to the shoe itself. The challenge here is the sequence of holes through which the lace must be threaded. This is where the parent must very slowly perform the actions and then encourage the child to continue what has been started. If using crisscross threading, the child must learn to swing left to right, then right to left, with each of the ends of the laces as it performs the threading sequence.

Tying a shoelace

Another difficult task, involving greater manual dexterity, is the actual tying of the laces having threaded them. Making a crisscross tie followed by looping ties is not easy and may take a great deal of practice. The task is made worse by the fact that it has to be done with the shoe already on the foot. The earlier task of lacing the shoes can be done with the shoes placed in a convenient position on a table, where the child can follow the sequence of actions very closely. But to tie up the shoe, he must crouch or bend over at the same time as performing the manual sequence.

Getting dressed

There is some evidence to suggest that boys find it harder than girls to master doing up buttons and opening and closing zip fasteners. This may be because boys generally tend to take less interest than girls in the business of dressing up and choosing and handling articles of clothing. This is probably largely a maternal influence, with mothers spending more time dressing up little girls. The result is that girls get more practice at buttoning.

age 2

What's happening inside and out

Brain
The brain is now about 80 per cent of its adult size. During this year, the frontal lobes (responsible for rational thoughts, planning and reasoning as well as emotions and memory) are developing at a much faster rate, which may help to explain the mood swings experienced by this age group.

Teeth
The full set of primary (baby) teeth will appear.

Average weight
Boys: 15 kg (33 lb)   Girls: 10.5 kg (23 lb)

Average height
Boys: 91 cm (36 in)   Girls: 81 cm (32 in)

Head circumference
Boys: 48.8 cm (19¼ in)   Girls: 47.8 cm (18¾ in)

Sleep requirements
12–14 hours

81 cm (32 in)   88 cm (34½ in)   94 cm (37 in)   101 cm (40 in)

the amazing world of twos and threes

Delightful and demanding, the child at this age is a wonder to behold, evolving from a still-uncertain, highly-egocentric toddler to a confident, sociable pre-schooler. The child's emotional world expands from the self to include a sense of relating to others, as well as a developing sense of personal identity. Imagination bursts into action, leading to plenty of questions, as well as newly discovered fears. She develops gross and fine motor skills, which now offer her the ability to climb, jump, run and draw. An age of blossoming independence, this is a time of intense learning and observation of the world around her, with every experience stored safely away amongst the increasingly connected network of the child's amazing developing brain.

≪ the child at 2

the child at 3 ≫

age 3

What's happening inside and out

Brain
By the age of 3, the child's brain is almost fully-grown and many neuron pathways are established, although each neuron (there are approximately 100 billion of them) can connect to almost 15,000 others, so there's still plenty of room for making new pathways.

Teeth
Full set of primary (baby) teeth have now grown.

Average weight
Boys: 17.25 kg (38 lb)   Girls: 11.5 kg (25 lb)

Average height
Boys: 100 cm (39½ in)   Girls: 88 cm (34½ in)

Head circumference
Boys: 49.8 cm (19½ in)   Girls: 48.9 cm (19¼ in)

Sleep requirements
11–13 hours

91 cm (36 in)   100 cm (39½ in)   109 cm (43 in)   117 cm (46 in)

At 2, the child is still unable to grasp the notion of others, so he may voice his protests if another person picks up his toys, looks through his books or gives his parents a hug. In his world, his objects are an extension of his self.

Shy or confident?
Between 10 and 20 per cent of children will be subdued and shy with strangers, while 20–40 per cent will be keen to approach the unfamiliar, and this tendency to either approach or withdraw from unfamiliar situations at 2 is a good indicator of what a child's temperament will be at school age. Studies have shown that 90 per cent of children who appeared uninhibited during their toddler years were also uninhibited at school age, while 60 per cent of those who were considered inhibited as toddlers remained that way at school age. It is believed that this tendency to approach or withdraw from social situations is linked to a more-reactive amygdala – the part of the brain that detects threats and triggers emotional responses.

the social and emotional world

The 2-year-old child wishes to be master and commander of his world and will prefer solitary play. He may watch and imitate other children, but he will rarely want to interact and finds the concept of taking turns highly puzzling. While he may want to be a part of everything and in control, he's also just discovering that the world is a challenging place that doesn't always do his bidding. When this happens, he may swiftly dissolve into a tantrum. This is all part of the maturation process as the child develops a sense of self in relation to others. Discipline and reason hold no sway, although humour and distraction will work wonders. During this year a child will gradually come to understand the benefits of cooperation. Despite his desire for independence, he is keenly aware of the absence of his main carer, and separation is still a major step for 2-year-olds.

It is at this age that a child will start to think about cause and effect. Solitary play allows a child the space for testing theories about all manner of things: What happens when I put one block on top of another block? And why do they all fall over when I put a third one on top?

the physical world of movement

Improving fine motor skills mean that she can now dress herself, as long as the buttons aren't too fiddly and there are no shoelaces to negotiate. She will now use a tricuspid grasp – holding her crayon between her thumb and two fingers – when drawing, and has much more control. She will use vertical and horizontal strokes in an intentional manner as well as making clear circular shapes. Helping to water the garden or cook in the kitchen may become popular now, as the 3-year-old is becoming skilled at pouring liquids and carrying containers.

Now much more confident, the 3-year-old child can walk up stairs using alternate feet. Marching, jumping, running and swinging have all been mastered, and she is even able to walk on tiptoes, albeit briefly.

Pretend play, such as picking up a banana and pretending it is a telephone, is a child's first steps toward abstract thought. Studies have shown that this kind of pretend play, which starts around the age of 2, is linked to social and linguistic ability. It tends to involve role playing, problem solving, interactive social dialogue and goal seeking, and engages many areas of the brain.

Learning to focus

At 2, the child is still developing the ability to mask out indiscriminate background noises from their environment in order to focus, which may be one of the reasons why various studies have found that young children's solitary play is disrupted by a television being on in the background. Researchers have also found that parents are less active, attentive and responsive, as well as talk to children about 20 per cent less, with a television on in the background.

The development of balance is a crucial stage for the 3-year-old child. Activities such as rocking, spinning or balancing on one foot all help to develop the cerebellum, which connects the vestibular system to the balance mechanism in the inner ear.

Up to the age of 3, boys tend to out-perform girls in visual-spatial exercises and certain types of hand-eye coordination, such as assembling jigsaw puzzles. That's because the right hemisphere of the brain – which is more involved in spatial exercises – is more active in boys, while girls tend to develop both hemispheres at an equal pace.

Time to take action

From the age of 3, a child can make sense of action words without the direct help of an adult. Researchers have found that while a child under 3 needs an adult to give her direct one-to-one guidance, over the age of 3 a child is perfectly capable of learning unfamiliar actions from watching a television programme, without having an adult available to give her additional support.

The 2-year-old can often be observed squatting for long periods while focused on his play. This is indicative of one of the neuromuscular developments stages that takes place between birth and 5, and is a crucial skill to practise in order to be able to move from lying down to standing.

Little athletes

What determines a child's athleticism? A small research study has now demonstrated that a parent's perception of their child's athletic ability, starting from around the age of 2, has a direct impact on how much a child participates in physical activity. Contrary to popular belief, a child is not as influenced by seeing his parents exercise as he is by the support, encouragement and opportunities he is given to try out a range of physical activities.

When you see a child transferring her crayon from one hand to the other while she is scribbling, she is demonstrating the 2-year-old's difficulty in moving one side of the body across the centre line of the body – otherwise known as crossing the midline. This is because, until the age of 3, the corpus callosum, which joins the left and right hemispheres of the brain, is still immature, making it difficult for the child to work across both sides of the body.

Why does the 3-year-old child ask so many questions? Well, apparently, it's because she really wants to know the answer. Children are active strategists when it comes to gleaning information about the world around them.

The benefits of lying

Lying demands quite advanced cognitive and social skills, which makes it a developmental milestone! Indeed, it has been shown that a child who starts lying at 3 will do better in intelligence tests later in life. By 4, almost all children will lie on a regular basis. However, the purpose of a 3-year-old's lie is quite different to that of a 4-year-old. At 3, a child will lie to avoid punishment; an older child will also lie as a way of controlling a social situation. Research has shown that teaching a child that honesty is something to be celebrated has a much greater impact on the 3-year-old who fears punishment than teaching him that dishonesty will be punished, as is the case in the commonly told 'Boy Who Cried Wolf' story.

language and learning

A 3-year-old's brain is twice as active as an adult brain, so it's not surprising that this is the age of questioning – everything. And with the 3-year-old's vocabulary now up to around 900 words, there are so many things to talk about. The 3-year-old child will also be happy to answer questions about what he is doing and what he is playing with. He might also talk quite a lot to himself as a way of acting out real-life situations. At 3, a child can conceptualize a timeline, so he can talk about past and future events. This complements another skill that develops this year – the ability to tell a simple story using sentences of up to five words. The 3-year-old also loves to hear stories, especially those that have an element of guessing or suspense. However, the child will still look puzzled if told a knock-knock joke, or stories involving puns or words with multiple meanings, as he still experiences words as having only one concrete meaning.

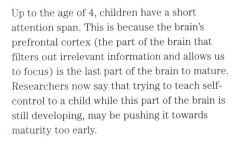

Up to the age of 4, children have a short attention span. This is because the brain's prefrontal cortex (the part of the brain that filters out irrelevant information and allows us to focus) is the last part of the brain to mature. Researchers now say that trying to teach self-control to a child while this part of the brain is still developing, may be pushing it towards maturity too early.

language and learning

At 2, the child has developed a more melodious way of speaking, with inflections that you may recognize as borrowed from a family member. With a vocabulary of between 50 and 300 words, she will be using verbs and adjectives to construct sentences of up to four words. The 2-year-old will still stumble over words, both because the mind is working faster than the mouth can physicalize, and also because certain phonetic combinations are difficult to vocalize (a blueberry is not a booberry, but it's temptingly close!). When alone, the 2-year-old may deliver a monologue lasting up to 15 minutes. This demonstrates the developing sense of self as she replays key experiences from her day. Although she still has a very short attention span, the 2-year-old will be able to follow instructions of up to three steps. The child at 2 may often be found simply staring into space pondering the nature of cause and effect, and is happy to play with intense concentration on self-selected activities for this very reason. However, this year also sees the start of imagination, and the 2-year-old will enjoy reading with an adult and talking about the characters.

The challenge of organizing visual information into ordered patterns is something the 2-year-old is now beginning to enjoy, although she can still only classify according to one defining principle. Asking her to sort out toys by colour, or the cars from the dolls, will keep her happily occupied (for a few minutes at least).

the social and emotional world

A huge amount of growth has occurred in the child's brain in the past year, and the result is that the 3-year-old will experience a year of relative calm. At 3, the child is increasingly aware of gender identity, and she will enjoy plenty of grown-up role play. Part of the joy of sharing is also the idea of being responsible, so having specific chores, like setting the table, will help the 3-year-old feel like she is contributing. This is also an age when rules start to offer some security – rather than a challenge – to a child and many things that may have been an issue in the previous year can be reconsidered, such as difficulties with eating, sleeping or tantrums. However, this is also the year when a child's imagination bursts into action, leading to plenty of questions as well as fears about both the world that the child can see and that is imagined.

Peer pressure

When it comes to deciding on who is right and who is wrong, 3-year-olds will go with the majority. Research has shown that when children are shown a series of individual adults being asked the name of a completely anonymous object, with one adult giving a different name than all the others, children will then answer the same question in accordance with the majority.

There will often be shifts in allegiance between parents at this age, with most 3-year-olds preferring the parent of the same gender. This preference is most likely to be because a child is learning about their world through role play and imitation.

Her sense of self has expanded to include a sense of others, and this inspires a new and delightful altruism; sharing, taking turns, empathy and cooperative play all become a natural part of the 3-year-old's repertoire. This makes it the ideal time for establishing shared family events, such as regular mealtimes and daily one-to-one time.

the physical world of movement

A 2-year-old's skill at motor-planning – the ability to plan, implement and then carry out a sequence of actions – develops dramatically during this year. The increasingly independent child can now start to do things and go places that were not previously possible. Kicking and throwing a large ball becomes a much-loved activity, as the larger muscle groups are now capable of controlling this action more effectively. However, the skill of catching a ball is still being acquired, as this requires a relatively sophisticated physical assessment of where the ball will land. He will still use two feet as he makes his way up and down stairs, although he will now be keen to do this independently. Climbing has also become a useful skill, as he can climb onto tables via chairs and into cupboards when he wants a particular book or toy.

This is the year when fine motor skills – those more intricate actions of the smaller muscle groups that require greater hand–eye coordination – really start to function. As a result, the 2-year-old can build towers of up to six blocks, and use a cup with two hands as well as a spoon and fork. She can also turn the pages of a book and hold a crayon – albeit with all five fingers clasped around the implement.

using scissors

One refined motor skill that adults take for granted is the use of scissors for cutting. This does not come naturally to a small child and has to be learned and refined. It may seem like a trivial activity, but it embodies some important learning skills.

Learning to cut

Cutting with scissors can be learnt as early as the age of 2, when a child should be able to snip the ends off a piece of paper. A 3-year-old child should be able to cut along a line marked on the paper. A 4-year-old should be able to cut out a circle that is marked on the paper. By 5 years of age, a child should be able to cut out a marked square, keeping the corners sharp.

When learning, thicker material is easier to cut than thin material. A young child may be able to cut through play dough before she can manage thick paper. After thick paper she can be tested on thin paper and finally on tissue paper – the most difficult of all.

There are special scissors with rounded ends that are more stable and less dangerous to use, but all scissor-cutting should be done in the presence of an adult, for reasons of safety.

The advantages of being able to cut

There are several advantages in learning to use scissors. The opening and closing of the blades of the scissors helps a child to strengthen the muscles in the palm of her hand. These muscles are also used in other daily activities such as holding a spoon, a fork, a toothbrush, a paintbrush, a pencil or a pen, so all of these activities may benefit.

Cutting also helps to improve hand-eye coordination. Such an action demands that the brain works with two systems at the same time – a visual one and a manual one. Again, this has many other applications, like catching a ball, fastening clothes or scooping up food.

Thirdly, cutting involves the improvement of bilateral coordination. When cutting a circle, for example, one hand turns the paper while the other does the physical cutting. The hands work at the same time but perform different manual actions. Once again, this is good training for many other common skills.

Left-handed scissors

The left-handed child sometimes finds herself at a disadvantage, because scissors are designed for right-handers. However, it is now possible to buy left-handed scissors, which have the left blade on top instead of the right blade, giving the left-hander a clear view of the cutting line. Also, the grip is moulded so that it is comfortable to fit around the joint of the left thumb.

swimming

In an ideal world, swimming is a skill that is learnt very early in life, even before schooldays have begun. A baby has an inborn ability to swim that soon vanishes and has to be replaced by learnt swimming actions. However, if a pre-school child has frequent access to warm water, she will find it much easier to learn to swim than if she starts at a later age.

The start of swimming

Small children who grow up in the coastal regions of tropical countries take to the water without any fears or preconceived ideas about swimming techniques. At the age of 3 they start splashing about in the shallows and, by the age of 4, both muscle power and physical coordination are well enough developed to allow them to make serious progress with a minimum of training. They simply play at being in the water, learning all the various possibilities of limb movement and progression. Swimming is fun and looked upon as just another game to play. They witness the superior swimming of their older companions and do their best to emulate them. There is no formal training, but by the time these children are older they will have become experts on their own terms.

Problems with swimming

The typical age for one of these 'coastal' children to swim a good distance unaided is 4½ years. For inland children living in colder climates the picture is very different. For them, swimming can become something of an ordeal. There are several factors working against them. The water in northern seas and lakes is usually too cold for the small body of a child, even in heated pools. Rivers are too dirty and too dangerous and most parents have little choice but to take their young children to public pools, where the chlorine can sting their eyes and overcrowding is often a problem. Also there are strict safety rules that make swimming lessons too much like a military training exercise rather than a joyous childhood game, and the water in which the young ones are being introduced to an entirely new form of locomotion is usually overcrowded with other bodies that keep getting in the way. It is not surprising to learn that, among British children no fewer than 35 per cent of them are totally unable to swim at the age of 11.

For them, one of the great delights of childhood has been turned into an unpleasant chore.

Swimming as play

For those parents who have the time and the energy to take their pre-school children swimming in a pleasant pool on a regular basis, and to make it a fun occasion rather than a stressful survival course, there are great rewards to be gained. The delight that a tiny child takes in flinging herself into the water, once she has mastered her fears, is a joy to behold. Once she has learnt how to float, surface and breathe when swimming, the freedom that the aquatic medium gives to muscular movements greatly extends the range of physical actions, especially limb movements, that a child can explore.

Safety can be dealt with by the use of inflatable armbands or rubber rings, until the child is ready to launch out on her own. Snorkel masks or swimming goggles can also be used if there is apprehension about putting the face below water. Racing contests, water polo and other competitive games help to divert the attention from the hazards and mechanics of swimming and allow it to develop naturally.

learning curves

the ability to learn

The human brain undergoes major developments during the first five years of life, making connections that will last a lifetime, and these changes are important for our understanding of the different ways a child's learning develops in the pre-school phase.

Types of learning

Children learn through observation, listening, practical experimentation and deduction. These processes are crucial to the way a young child's brain organizes connections from experiences, and critical periods for making these connections have been recognized as occuring in the pre-school years. There are five main ways in which a child learns:

Repetitive practice
Trial and error
Copying more experienced individuals
Thinking about a problem and working it out
Listening to and following instructions

Of these five procedures, the first four can be managed by our cousins, the apes. Imagine a banana hanging up high in a chimpanzee's cage. At first the ape jumps up to reach it, but fails. The ape then jumps again and again, until it has improved its vertical leap through repetitive practice and manages to snatch the banana. Alternatively, it may try out several different kinds of leap – a standing leap, a crouching leap, a running leap, and so on, until it finds one method that, by trial and error, enables it to snatch the banana. Thirdly, it may watch an old ape use the wire netting of the cage next door to give it a higher leap and then copy this action itself. Fourthly, the ape may sit down on the floor, scratch its chin in frustration and then, spotting some boxes in its cage, reason that if they were piled up on top of one another it could climb high enough to reach the banana. However, if a zookeeper comes along and tells the ape to solve the problem by asking for a long stick to knock the banana down, the animal will not understand what he is saying, nor will it be able to ask.

Unlike the ape, the pre-school child is capable of all five of these types of learning. They will not, however, all appear at the same time in the journey from 2 to 5 years of age. Sitting down to think out a problem before acting is a later arrival than practice, trial and error and imitation. Learning by instruction depends on how far verbal language has developed. For the 2-year-old the instructions have to be very simple. For the 5-year-old they can be much more sophisticated.

The learning environment

Three preferred learning styles have been identified: visual, such as flash cards; auditory, such as singing or storytelling; and kinaesthetic, such as acting with toys or props. This variety of learning methods helps stimulate different senses and encourage brain plasticity.

The environment has a huge impact on the way in which a child learns. Of course, some kinds of training have to be carried out with caution and careful control, but those that can be achieved in a playful way, without any pressure, are the ones that give the child the most pleasure. A simple mathematical problem, presented coldly, has little appeal, but the same problem disguised as an amusing game is learned with far less trouble. Every small child is, by nature, a compulsive problem-solver and watching him struggling to reach his goals and finally achieve a minor triumph is one of the great privileges of parenthood.

theories about learning

It was not until the 20th century that serious attention was paid to the psychological development of the child during the earliest phases of her life. Then several major theories were put forward, stressing slightly different aspect of the process. Three of the most famous were those of Jean Piaget, Erik Erikson and John Watson.

Piaget's theories

Jean Piaget was a Swiss psychologist who developed a theory of child intelligence that saw each phase of childhood being dominated by certain particular forms of thinking and acting. The pre-school phase from 2 to 6 years of age was one that he called the Pre-operational Stage, central to which was the rapid acquisition of language. Language, of course, involves symbolic thinking, in which one thing stands for another. The word 'tree' does not look like a real tree, but it comes to mean a tree nonetheless. Linked to this, is the child's development of symbolic acting, in which she pretends that a cushion is a horse that she is riding, or that a cardboard box is a motorcar. Role play also develops during this phase, with a child acting the part of someone else – he is the train driver and you are one of his passengers (see Role Play, pages 96–97).

While these patterns of behaviour become active during the pre-school phase, others do not. Piaget stresses, for example, the fact that pre-school children are all egocentric and almost unable to see someone else's point of view. In a famous test, he showed a picture of a mountain to a group of children and asked them to select a picture from several views of the same mountain. The children had to choose a view that would have been seen by someone else, from a different viewpoint. Surprisingly, they always chose their own view of the mountain, revealing that, in their opinion, only their view mattered.

Piaget was later criticized, because he did not base his conclusions on a large enough sample of children. Later research revealed that, by the age of 4 or 5, children do start thinking about other people's views and are often less egocentric than Piaget suggested. His main stages of development may be correct, but they cannot be applied rigidly. There will always be some children who are late developers and others who start early. The richness of the environment in which they are growing up has a lot to do with this and this was recognized by the research of Lev Vygotsky, who offered an alternative to Piaget's theory, suggesting that children develop through social interaction.

Erikson's theories

Erik Erikson was a German psychoanalyst who rejected Sigmund Freud's bizarre ideas about infant sexuality and replaced them with a more useful theory of psychosocial stages of development. He saw the period from 2 to 5 years in two main stages, the first of which he called Psychosocial Stage 2. In this phase of development (age 2 to 3) the child struggles to learn how to control her body. When moving about, her limbs still do not do quite what she wants them to do, causing frustration. Bowel and bladder actions are also not fully controlled. The more the child can control her actions and movements, the more independent she can feel. She struggles to put behind her the baby phase of total dependence.

Psychosocial Stage 3 (age 3 to 5) is seen more as a time for exploration, when the child asserts the controls she has achieved. She often tries to take the lead in social activities and play and, if successful, feels a great sense of personal achievement. By the time she goes to school, the child has already become either a leader or a follower.

Watson's theories

John Watson was an American psychologist who believed in the ruthless training of children. He was interested only in their outward behaviour and not in their welfare, their inner thoughts or their feelings. He saw each child as the subject of experiments involving punishments and rewards,

and argued that he could train any child to grow up to be any kind of adult. He even experimented on children, creating the fear of white rats in one child by playing terrifying sounds every time the child saw a rat. He also showed that this child had developed fears of other small white furry objects.

In the Watsonian scheme of behaviour, every child was to be treated like a small adult, subordinate to your will, and moulded to suit your convenience. If a child was crying with misery, Watson recommended that she be left to cry herself out, so that she would discover that she had no power to influence her parents or anyone else. Watson's teachings, which were treated seriously in the 1920s and 1930s did untold harm. Today they are largely ignored, although every so often someone appears on the scene, who tries to reinstate these extreme views.

Recent theories

In recent years more theories have been put forward focusing on the influence of environmental factors on development. These ecological theories take into account the circumstances in which children live, their economic stability, family arrangements – whether single parent or divorced, for example – the size of the family, and so on. Advances in science have also helped to investigate the importance of genetically determined development stages. These biological theories consider the timings when a child is ready to move on to the next stage, for example sitting unaided or standing.

It has been suggested that children develop by processing the information from their environment, storing and retrieving it when required (see Processing Information, pages 72–73). As the child gets older these processes become more complex and integrated, forming their long-term memory.

It is clear that the ways in which children learn are complex, but by providing a stimulating environment and recognizing the natural stages of growth, parents and teachers are encouraging the developing brain.

processing information

A child's pre-school years may be filled with light-hearted play, but her brain is far from idle. There is so much input arriving, so many novel experiences presenting themselves, hour by hour, that the brain cells are kept busy working overtime doing their best to process, sort and store all this new information.

The stages of processing

Some theorists liken the way children process information to a computer. There are four stages of processing new information: input, integration, storage and output. Input sees the latest experiences reach the brain via the sense organs: the eyes, the ears, the nose, the tongue and the touch-sensitive skin. The vast majority of new input comes though the eyes, with the ears second. Integration sees this new information sorted and related to previous information that is already present in the brain. New experiences have to be interpreted and then classified. Once they have been placed in a particular category and arranged in a particular sequence, they are then ready to be filed away. Storage of new information involves placing it in a memory bank. It may end up as a short-term memory, available for present use, or be more deeply embedded in long-term memory and, from there, available for the future. Output is the reuse of the stored memories and their employment in some form of action. Actions appear in the form of gestures, manipulations, locomotion and other muscular movements, nonverbal sound utterances, such as shouts or cries, verbal speech, written words or drawn images.

Inputting new information

The brain is not capable of processing all the experiences its sense organs are sending to it. When a child enters a room she is not capable of responding to everything she sees there. If she did so, her behaviour would be chaotic. She must learn to be selective and to focus on one thing at a time. Some children are better at this than others. With sound information, for example, those that have input difficulties may find it hard to screen out the irrelevant noise and cut through the playgroup hubbub to concentrate on the teacher's voice. Other children may have defective hearing or vision without being aware of it. At this very young age a child may find it hard to express the fact that she cannot hear clearly or enjoy sharp vision and she has nothing with which to compare her sensory abilities. Today most children are tested for these problems.

Sorting new information

The child's brain, having received information from the sense organs, must decide what to keep and what to discard. One of the problems at this point is caused by new input being too complicated, making it difficult for the child to tease out the essential elements she wants to retain. A good teacher, or a sensitive parent, presents new experiences in such a way that they start simply, gradually becoming more complex. The child's brain can build new understanding bit by bit, each new element being easier to accept because of the earlier ones that are already there.

Storing new information

Once the new input has been sorted and irrelevant details discarded, the information received must be stored away in the brain for future reference. There are three important stages in this process. First, the new information must be stored fleetingly in the sensory register. It is then passed on to the workspace of the brain where it is held as short-term memory. There it can be thought about and decisions can be made about how important it is. If it is felt to be a highly significant new piece of information it may then be transferred to the long-term memory. This is the encyclopaedia of the mind to which we turn when we need to retrieve a fact, an image or an idea.

testing intelligence

Intelligence is a quality that should not be confused with knowledge, creativity or motivation. Knowledge is how much information you already have inside your head. Creativity is how imaginative and inventive you are (see The Creative Child, pages 106–107). And motivation is how much mental energy you have. The correct definition of intelligence is the ability to use old information to solve new problems.

The validity of intelligence tests

Intelligence tests have often be criticized as being relatively useless, because they tend to ignore creativity and motivation. Criticism also suggests that it is possible to become expert at doing them. A child given many such tests soon gets used to the kind of questions asked. Therefore, the parent who repeatedly sets his child intelligent tests at home gives his offspring an unfair advantage over others when official tests are eventually carried out.

The circumstances under which tests are carried out have also been criticized. If the tests are done at home, where children are relaxed and under no pressure, they may do much better than if they are examined under more formal conditions in an unfamiliar setting. Also, those children who are less sensitive to being in a strange place may do better than those who are timid. So the formal tests are, again, said to be unfair. What they are really testing, it is claimed, is personality type – a lack of timidity rather than true intelligence.

It was once believed that intelligence was fixed at birth, but contemporary theories hold the notion that intelligence can change over time and that nurture is more influential than nature in the hereditary versus environment debate – it is now thought that 40 per cent of our intelligence is influenced by genes, and 60 per cent by the environment.

The Wechsler test

Intelligence tests still have their place and can reveal something useful about the relative brightness of a child. One of the best-known tests for pre-school children is the Wechsler Pre-school and Primary Scale of Intelligence.

This consists of three verbal tests: general information; definitions of words; and guessing the meaning of a word from one, two or three clues. Next there are three performance tests: copying small geometric designs; completing designs that have missing parts; and choosing from several rows of pictures, those that have common characteristics. Finally, there are two speed tests: copying symbols that are paired with simple geometric designs; and searching for target symbols in a row of symbols.

The most valuable use of intelligence tests of this sort is not to identify champion testers with the highest IQ (Intelligence Quotient), but rather to single out any child who has unusual difficulties and may therefore be suffering from a serious learning problem that requires specialist help. Without such tests, a backward child may not be identified soon enough to enable concerned adults to address his particular dilemma at an early stage.

Creativity tests

Intelligence tests have been around long enough for people to have noticed that those with the highest IQ are not necessarily the most successful members of society. They may be able to solve complex puzzles and word games, and they may even possess a great deal of general knowledge, but something is clearly lacking. They may not have a strong enough motivation to utilize their intelligence, or they may lack the imagination to employ it productively.

This, once again, brings up the question of creativity. In recent years there has been a greater interest in this quality and there are now creativity tests as well as intelligence tests. These ask a different kind of question, in which the goal is to test originality.

Examples of creativity test challenges include thinking of as many words as possible that contain a specified letter of the alphabet; naming as many examples of a class of things as possible (types of toy, names of girls, farm animals); the number of possible uses that can be found for a particular object (like a bucket, a brick, or a ball); elaborating a particular shape on a piece of paper into something else. Tests of this kind examine what is called divergent thinking – finding as many answers as possible to a single question, whereas with intelligence testing there is only one correct answer.

gifted and talented

Every so often, a child shows an unusually rapid increase in intellectual ability. Physically, socially and emotionally she is still very young, but her intellect races ahead and soon reaches a stage similar to that seen in much older children. At first sight this seems to be a blessing, both for the child and for her parents, but because she is out of step with the other children of her age, being gifted can also cause problems that are difficult to solve.

The dilemma of the gifted child

The gifted child is the one who always comes top of her class. It has been estimated that, in a typical classroom of children, there is on average one child who can be classified as gifted. Although physically the same as the rest of her group, and just as immature as them in emotional development and social skills, she discovers herself to be surprisingly much more intelligent. She probably encounters lavish praise from her parents and her teachers for being so advanced, but finds this rather difficult to understand, because she sees herself, not as abnormally successful, but simply as normal, with her friends appearing to be rather backward.

What happens to this gifted child? If she is placed in a special class along with other gifted children, they become an elite group, looked upon as oddities. If she stays in her old class, one of two things can happen. If she is an outgoing child she will become overtly precocious and possibly even arrogant. It is not her fault, but if she keeps hearing how clever she is, this is bound to affect her attitudes to others. At the pre-school stage there is a serious risk that she may become a bumptious show-off and this may lead to her becoming isolated and unpopular.

If she is, instead, a quiet, reserved child, she will try hard not to become different from her friends, and will therefore do everything she can to hide her superior intelligence. This will cause another kind of problem because she will feel increasingly bored with the challenges that she finds much too easy. For her, conforming to the norm may become a major frustration.

Helping the gifted child

The secret to helping the gifted child solve her dilemma is to recognize her thirst for knowledge and to keep feeding it without her becoming a show-off or bored and frustrated. This is not easy, but with sensitivity it can be done. One advantage is that, if a child is unusually intelligent, it is possible for a parent to explain, even at a very young age, that her less advanced friends may become envious and even hostile if they are made to feel inferior. If the gifted child can understand this, it is then possible for the parents to set up, almost as a secret game, an outlet for expressing the young one's brilliance. In the privacy of the home they can foster the child's special demands for mental stimulation in one area or another. She may be able to satisfy her intellectual needs by becoming clever at chess, for example, or by advanced reading with her parents, or solving mathematical puzzles, or in some other way. Then, when with her friends, she can knowingly play down her abilities without feeling too frustrated.

The talented child

The talented child is different from the gifted child. Instead of a general superiority in intelligence, she has one particular creative ability, such as playing a musical instrument, singing, or acting and dancing. A talented child of this sort is usually no more intelligent than her friends and finds it easier to rub along with the rest of them in day-to-day situations, showing off her unusual talents only on special occasions or in the privacy of her home.

thought processes

There is an old country saying: 'Sometimes I sits and thinks and sometimes I just sits'.
Careful thought is not the pre-schooler's most favoured method of solving a problem.
He much prefers a physically active approach to a philosophical one. If he is observed
apparently deep in thought, there is a good chance that he has, for a moment, allowed his
brain to go 'off-line' or perhaps daydream and is not sitting and thinking, but just sitting.

The limitations

The thinking processes of the very young are often fanciful
and lacking in cold logic. Toys can become real friends, the
fact that they are made of cloth or wood doing nothing to
interfere with this mode of thought. Simple tests of logic
can also produce some surprising results that reveal the big
difference that exists between the ways that pre-school
children and adults think. The child often focuses on only
one aspect of a situation and ignores others. A famous
example is the water-level test. If a 4-year-old is shown two
glass containers – one tall and thin and the other wide and
low – and each holding the same amount of water, he will
notice the way in which the water level in the tall thin
container is much higher than that in the wide shallow
container. If he is asked which container holds the most
water, he will unhesitatingly indicate the tall vessel.

In another version of the same test, if the 4-year-old is
given the two glass containers empty, and asked to fill them
up so that they each contain the same amount of water, he
will fill them up until the level in the tall one is the same
height as the level in the wide one. If an older sibling, say
a 7-year-old sister, watches him doing this, she will think
that what he has done is unbelievably stupid. Between the
ages of 4 and 7 the child's brain starts to think out problems
of this kind in a more complex way, taking into account
several qualities of the water and the container – in this
case its height. Reacting to more and more aspects of a
problem is one of the ways in which human thinking
progresses as the years pass.

Magical thinking

As adults, we are able to enjoy the drama of a fantasy while,
at the same time, knowing that it is untrue. Below the age

of 6 this is not always the case. Given a fairy tale or some
other kind of fable or folk legend, the pre-school child may
believe every word of it – Santa Claus really does come
down the chimney of every house with presents for
Christmas morning. A child trusts adults to tell him the
truth and accepts magical ideas as easily as he accepts
mundane facts. All over the world, small children sit
enthralled by tales of wonderful happenings, of children
who can fly, animals who can talk and dragons who breathe
fire. In their thinking, all such stories are valid, no matter
how strange they may seem. This provides a child with
hours of innocent pleasure that will only come to an end
when, at a slightly older age, he begins to apply cold logic
and reason to such matters, and sort fact from fiction. For
some individuals, of course, this progress to logical thinking
is never fully realized and, although they no longer believe
that there are fairies at the bottom of their garden, they do
retain infantile thought processes regarding such myths as
flying saucers and crop circles.

Everything has a purpose

The way in which the very young child thinks about the
purpose of things differs markedly from that of an adult.
Adults make a clear distinction between things that are
designed with a specific function in mind and those that
are not. Children often fail to make this distinction. For
example, a child, like an adult, thinks that a clock is
designed to allow us to tell the time, but a child will also
believe that a cloud is designed to give us rain. As the child
grows older, he eventually comes to distinguish between
things that are man-made with a specific purpose and those
natural phenomena that are not. As with the distinction
between magical and logical thinking, this distinction only
arrives after formal schooling has started.

states of consciousness

A child's body language provides vital clues to one of five mental states of awareness: alert consciousness, downtime, daydreaming, trance and sleep. The younger the child, the harder it is for her to concentrate, and if she is distracted for more than a few minutes she may forget what she was thinking about just moments before.

Alert consciousness

In this state, a child is actively receiving messages from the outside world, using some or all of her senses – hearing, sight, touch, smell and taste. Her body is constantly busy as she responds to sensations and processes information. Her posture varies according to how interested or relaxed she feels and her breathing and heart rate are closely linked to what she is doing. If she is concentrating hard, she will most likely push internal feelings to one side for the time being.

Downtime

There are times when a child is quiet and simply doesn't feel like chatting. That is fine and should not become a source of confrontation. She may be tired after a long day, or she may just need some downtime to process information and put her thoughts in order. This state of reflective consciousness occurs regularly throughout the day. Babies do it repeatedly and for long periods of time. In older children, the downtime periods are shorter and more widely spaced.

The most obvious sign that a child is entering downtime is that she will stop whatever she is doing, tilt her head and look away, sometimes only momentarily. Her involuntary eye movements indicate that she is analyzing something. Even from birth she looks in one direction, to the right or the left, most of the time. A sudden intake of breath may signal realization, while breathing out deeply is usually a sign of understanding.

Daydreaming

When a deeper level of thought is required, the body slows down some of its functions and a child ignores outside distractions. But although she may be oblivious to what is going on, she is still fully conscious and able to react to outside stimuli if necessary. A daydreaming child may stare into the distance. While she does this, her feet may start tapping, she may display subtle tongue or throat movements as she rehearses conversations, and her eyes may flicker as she sees things in her imagination.

Trance

At an even deeper level, an almost trance-like state may occur. This is often obvious when a child is watching television and trying to make sense of what is happening on the screen. The gaze is defocused, the child may even close her eyes and her facial expression is blank. In this state she is silent or her speech is slow and hesitant. Her pulse, blink rate and breathing rate are reduced. The trance-like state may also occur when a child is unwell, in which case she may look pale or be flushed and perspiring.

Sleep

The final state of deep thought processing occurs when a child is in dream sleep. After the first period of deep sleep, the child enters the first stage of dream sleep accompanied by rapid eye movements below flickering eyelids. All body processes are slowed down and the body is generally relaxed, although there might be some slight body movement and occasional talking in her sleep.

perception

Perception is the way the brain interprets all the information coming to it from the child's senses – vision, sounds, smell, taste and touch. Perception is still developing throughout the pre-school phase and with some children the process is much slower than with others. Children differ from adults in the way they perceive the world around them, and these differences are often overlooked by parents.

Developing perception

Perception can be described as what a person understands from their senses. Information from the senses is processed in the brain, where it is compared with stored information. The brain either reacts automatically or formulates a more considered response. The basic reactions are in place in the newborn but the more advanced responses are refined as the child develops. Developmental milestones help to gauge the stage that a child has reached in refining his senses and interpreting the information he receives.

Visual perception

Refining visual perception is an important part of mental development between the ages of 2 and 5. Five skills have been identified:

Form recognition: for example being able to recognize that a shape that has been turned on its side is still the same form.

Visual closure: for example, being able to guess what a final picture will be when only part of it is visible.

Sequential memory: for example, being able to remember a sequence of units, such as a telephone number.

Spatial memory: for example, being able to remember the location of a hidden object.

Searching image: for example, being able to ignore irrelevant details when searching visually for a particular type of object.

A child with learning difficulties may have problems with one or more of these skills, but the typical pre-school child develops all these abilities to the point where they become so automatic that he does not have to think about them consciously.

The precise understanding of tiny details in the visual field is an important factor in the development of reading and writing. A small percentage of children have difficulties in this respect and are referred to as being dyslexic. Although intelligent in other respects, these children usually find reading and writing difficult.

Sound signals

Adults rarely take into account the fact that the hearing of a small child is more sensitive than their own. It is more sensitive both in pitch and volume. Pitch is measured in hertz (hz), a standardized term for 'cycles per second', and the ears of the pre-school child can detect sounds as high-pitched as 20,000 hz or more. From about the age of 8, this range starts to shrink, with the higher frequencies fading, so that an adult's range ends up considerably lower, somewhere around 15,000 or 16,000 hz. This decline in hearing sensitivity is normal and applies to all humans.

The preferred sound volume for a small child is up to about 20 decibels, with a maximum of 35 decibels for a child with normal hearing. Tests have shown that the decibel level in a noisy playgroup in a large, echoing room may be as high as 55 to 75 decibels – far beyond what is pleasant for the ears of a very young child. This may account for part of the problem when a timid child is introduced to his first playgroup. What may seem an exciting hubbub to those who have become accustomed to it, may sound like bedlam to his sensitive hearing system.

Studies of children living in a noisy environment (near an airport for example) have revealed that the way in which they cope with the high level of sound is by training themselves to disregard auditory input. Unfortunately, this means that they also tend to tune out human speech. The result is that their reading abilities, and any other abilities involving tasks that require speech perception, suffer.

Perceiving odours

As with other senses, adults frequently make mistakes about how they imagine the young child perceives odours, assuming that if something smells good or bad to them it must also smell good or bad to the young one. This is not the case. Surprisingly, perhaps, careful experiments revealed that children aged 2, 3 and 4, usually do not find the smell of faeces or sweat unattractive. This changes dramatically at the age of 5, when these odours are suddenly responded to as deeply unpleasant, a response that lasts until extreme old age when the sensory systems start to shut down again.

Other differences also exist. Tests have proven that young children do not appreciate flowery smells or, say, petrol as much as adults do. In the opposite direction, children are much more appreciative of fruity and nutty smells than are adults.

Perceiving taste

Children have more taste buds than adults and are highly sensitive to the flavours of different kinds of foods. A major difference is that there is a much stronger preference for sweet tastes and a stronger dislike for other tastes. In this respect, the pre-school child is intermediate between a baby and an adult. A baby likes only sweet tastes and an adult likes a wide variety of tastes. Infantile sweetness is still favoured by the small child, but he is also prepared to start trying out other flavours.

the nature of language

The ability to talk to one another gives human beings their greatest evolutionary advantage. Chimpanzees can manufacture tools, engage in social strategies and even participate in group hunting expeditions, but they cannot talk. Symbolic spoken language is our crowning glory and it has made us what we are today. In the past, it was generally supposed that the language abilities of the small child were entirely the result of adult teaching, that every step he took towards efficient verbal communication was due solely to the efforts of his parents or other adults. In recent years this view has been modified slightly.

An innate urge to talk

If the acquisition of language in small children owes everything to adult teaching, then we might expect to see huge differences in different cultures. True, we do see many different languages as we move from country to country, but the remarkable feature of these various tongues is that they all have a very similar basic structure and grammar. They may have different nouns and verbs and adjectives, but they all arrange them in much the same way and construct sentences in a similar fashion. What is more, this basic grammar is acquired at the same age and the same speed in all cultures. Between the ages of 2 and 5, the number of words known increases at the same rate: a 4-year-old Vietnamese will have a vocabulary of about the same size as a 4-year-old Norwegian. And in all cultures there will be an almost magical rush towards articulate

speech that progresses at an amazing pace during the pre-school years. There can only be one conclusion from this, namely that the human species has an innate 'language acquisition device'.

This was the controversial view put forward by the American linguist Noam Chomsky in the mid-20th century, when he proposed a 'universal grammar' to explain the inexplicably rapid pace at which all children learn languages. Expressed in simple terms, his idea was that, although individual words must be learned from parents or other adults, the way they are used and mixed together to make sentences is the result of a genetically inherited, inborn mechanism in the brain of the human child. Without such a device, he argued, it would be impossible for children the world over, at the same age and at the same high speed, to construct a grammar to utilize the learnt words. What is more, in the very early stages when they are struggling to develop and refine this unique communication skill, very small children all seem to make the same sorts of error, regardless of which tongue they are speaking. Other errors that one might expect to hear are strangely absent.

To find an analogy, if the brain of the child contains an inborn language 'tree' with dividing roots and branches, then the words that he learns are like leaves that enter his brain and become attached to this tree, making it a functional whole. French leaves will be different from German leaves or Italian leaves, but the basic structure of the tree will be the same in all cases. In previous language theories it had been suggested that all parts of the tree were brought in from the outside by learning from adults, but the chances of this happening across the entire globe are very unlikely.

So the tiny human child, uttering its very first 'mama' and 'dada' words is, in reality, a magnificent language-acquisition machine at the very beginning of an astonishing, internally-fuelled journey of extraordinary significance. Indeed, if we were looking for a new title for our species, perhaps the most appropriate one would be that of the 'talking ape'.

how language develops

There is a great deal of variation in the speed with which children develop their language skills, but there are some general guidelines to the progress that the typical child makes between the ages of 2 and 5. If a particular child is slower than average she soon catches up at a later age. The more that parents talk to children, using their normal adult voices and avoiding the temptation to employ 'baby talk', the quicker their children will learn.

Early days

The typical 2-year-old has a vocabulary of between 150 and 300 words, while slow starters may only have about 50 words at this stage. One of the pleasures for the child at this early age is being able to name common objects in the rooms in which she lives. Three-word sentences are possible now, usually with a noun and a verb. Pronouns are being added, with the child signifying that she is talking about herself, or something connected to herself, by employing words such as 'me' 'my' 'mine' and 'I'. The correct use of 'I' and 'me' is not always in evidence, however, and these two words may be muddled up for a while yet.

Descriptions of the positions of objects begin to occur, with the use of such words as 'under' 'on' or 'in'. Some words that are already understood may not yet be used. If a 2-year-old is asked to touch a part of her body – her hair, ear, mouth and so on – she may be able to do this even though she has not yet started to speak those words when actively talking.

Vocabulary building

The typical 3-year-old has a vocabulary of between 500 and 1,000 words. She knows her name, her age and her sex. She can understand many questions but may not be able to answer all of them verbally. Her utterances are getting longer, and three-word sentences are now commonplace. The confusion between 'I' and 'me' is now resolved and she will understand and use plurals and past tenses. Language is starting to become a joy rather than a struggle.

Running commentary

The typical 4-year-old loves to talk when she is playing games. She enjoys the use of language so much that she may give a running commentary on what is happening to her toys as she moves them around. She may use words now to augment her make-believe play. And she may repeat words and phrases over and over again, as if practising them and listening to their sound. She has greater understanding of verbal concepts and opposites – longer and shorter, larger and smaller, over and under. She is also getting much better at identifying classes of objects. She can name many animals, colours, foods, and when she reads picture books she is able to put words to many of the illustrations. If long words are spoken to her she can, with concentration, repeat them – up to four syllables. And if a four-digit number is said to her slowly, she should be able to memorize and repeat it.

Everyday conversation

At 5 years old, the child has reached the stage at which speech becomes grammatical, with much longer sentences and descriptive words added to both nouns and verbs. The idea of time is now much better expressed, with today, tomorrow, yesterday; now, later, earlier; morning, afternoon, evening and night – all becoming part of her everyday conversation. Numbers are also better handled and serious counting skills are now enjoyed. This is a delightful age for conversations between child and parent and a magical time for shared moments of verbal communication of a freshness and innocence that will never be equalled at later stages of development.

speaking and listening

Learning and understanding words is not the same as being able to say them out loud in a way that others can understand. Diction is strongly influenced by the way the child hears adults speaking and a local dialect or accent soon begins to show. Some children find it difficult to make themselves heard and others may suffer from stuttering or stammering.

Speaking clearly

The urge to communicate by speaking rushes ahead of the ability to articulate clearly. The 2-year-old is liable to gabble and jabber away happily. At this stage about one-third of the words cannot be interpreted by others. The child's voice is poorly controlled – the pitch and volume both varying – and the rhythm of the words far from perfect.

By the age of 3, when a child talks to his parents, they can understand almost everything he says. Now, only about 10 per cent of his words are impossible to decipher. Clarity of speech then gradually improves until, by the age of 5, all his words can be understood.

The art of listening

We tend to think of talking as active and listening as passive, but this is a mistake, especially with young children. When a tiny child, having recently discovered the joy of speaking, talks earnestly to his mother, she may just pretend to be listening if her mind is really somewhere else. However, children, even the very young, are remarkably sensitive to this pretence of listening. If repeated too often, the child knows intuitively that what he has to say is of no real importance. Eventually he loses interest in his attempts at verbal communication and resorts to talking to himself.

Listening seriously to the chatter of a small child, and interacting with him in a spontaneous way, can make a huge difference to his development of language skills. It is also important that the child himself learns to listen patiently. For this to succeed, the parent must have something to say that interests the child – a perfect time for storytelling. Told dramatically, a good story can keep a child listening intently for a long period and this marks the start of genuine conversational listening in later life.

Gabbling, stuttering and stammering

Some children have a delivery problem with words. Some talk too fast as they fear that nobody will listen to them for very long, their words running into one another so badly that they are hard to follow. The cause is usually the impatience of busy adults trying to make time for their offspring. A child senses that his conversation period is limited and tries to squash everything he wants to say into as short a time span as possible. It may take several years for such a fault to correct itself.

Stuttering, or stammering, is the opposite. Known as 'verbal non-fluency', this speech defect prevents the child from getting the words he wants to say out of his mouth at the speed he wishes to utter them. He faces three problems as he tries to speak. He may find it impossible to bring out a word at all and experiences a dramatic, unwanted pause. Or he may start to utter a word but be unable to finish it, repeating the start of the word over and over again in rapid succession. Or he may be able to make a sound but finds it is drawn out into an abnormally long version.

Stuttering is not uncommon in 3- to 5-year-olds, as they learn to become more articulate, and it increases when they are stressed. In most cases it lasts only a few months. This is known as pseudo-stuttering and is nothing to worry about. If it continues or gets worse, it may develop into rare adult stuttering, and will require the help of a speech therapist. But at the very early stages of language development it is simply a learning phase in the process of becoming articulate. The worst way to deal with it is to interrupt the child or comment on the difficulty he is having. This only increases the tension, making the impediment worse. Patience and a calm atmosphere are the best solutions. Proof of this is that small children do not stutter when talking quietly to their toys.

play and games

Play is the dominant feature of pre-school life, its significance all too often underestimated. Between the ages of 2 and 5, the child lives to play. Sleeping, eating, drinking, washing and travelling are little more than interruptions in a magical world of playful investigation, exploration, inquisitiveness and the satisfaction of curiosity. Humans are the most playful beings on earth, and the pre-school phase is by far the most playful stage of human life.

Love of the new

Every parent knows that a new toy is the most exciting one. Unpacking it, examining it, trying it out, learning how much it will do, and then playing with it, provides a peak of excitement. The human brain is programmed to seek out novelty and explore it. After a while the new toy becomes too familiar and loses some of its appeal. Its possibilities exhausted, it is put aside and an older toy that has not been given much attention recently is brought out instead. The child's attention switches from one toy to the next; the longer a toy is ignored the more its novelty factor regains some strength.

Not all toys have equal appeal as play objects. The toy that offers the greatest variability is inevitably the one that is given most attention. A swing is popular because it provides a back-and-forth movement that can be made lower or higher. But apart from variations in the strength of each swing, it is a rather monotonous activity and does not last very long. A trampoline allows more variation in the up-and-down bouncing movements and is therefore more attractive. A pedal car or a tricycle has even more appeal because, although the child's action is a monotonous circling of the feet on the pedals, the result of these actions, combined with the turning of a steering wheel, gives endless possibilities. The child can now go here, there and anywhere that parents will allow (see Riding a Bike, pages 52–53). Ball play offers a similar degree of variability. The kicking or throwing action may not vary very much, but because of the spherical shape of the ball it can move in a thousand different directions (see Ball Play, pages 50–51). Each type of toy, therefore, has a 'novelty potential' based on the variability of the actions that are possible with it.

The games children play

A special form of play involves the invention or copying of a simple set of rules. A child may invent his own game, such as hiding his toys and asking a parent to hunt for them. The rules here are no more than that the parent must shut his eyes, and perhaps count, while the hiding takes place. Other games, suggested by parents or older children, such as hide-and-seek or musical chairs, are also eagerly adopted and may be played time and again until the child tires of them. Eventually, repetition will wear them out as novelties and they will have to be replaced with other themes. Some old favourites may keep putting in an appearance, especially those that are still enjoyed by older siblings.

As the months pass, puzzles, board games, card games, drawing and painting begin to be enjoyed, but these have limited appeal to the pre-school child because they involve prolonged periods of sitting down when there is so much physical energy demanding an outlet. However, after an exhausting bout of boisterous action-play, they are acceptable as fillers for quietening down periods.

Social play

Most early play is either solitary or carried out with the cooperation of the parents. Later on in the journey from 2 to 5 years, social play with other children of the same age begins to become more important. This may involve some sort of game with rules, or be purely physical, with activities like chasing, hiding and play fighting. There is always a risk with this physical type of play that, by accident, one child gets hurt, the laughter stops and a serious fight breaks out. This is, however, extremely rare and careful studies have revealed that it only occurs in about one per cent of all play fights. It is much more common for an accidental, minor injury to result in rough-and-tumble play being halted. Even at an early age, children are extremely good at making a clear distinction between play actions and serious ones.

using the imagination

Between the ages of 2 and 5, play that involves pretending is increasingly important in the life of a child. The boy pretends that the piece of wood in his hand is an aeroplane and plays at flying it around his room. The girl pretends that the doll she is holding is a real baby and plays at feeding it with imaginary food. Pretend play of this kind can be both solitary and social.

Double knowledge

In the cases mentioned above, neither child is fooled by what he or she is doing. Even as the boy flies his plane, making engine noises, he is aware that it is really only a piece of wood. And as the girl spoons imaginary food into her doll's mouth, saying 'eat up', she knows that she is not holding a real baby. This 'double knowledge' is the essence of pretend play. The child understands both the real and the imagined property of the toys. This is the beginning of symbolic thinking, of making one thing stand for another – an ability that becomes vitally important as the child grows. It is the basis of language, where a word is made to stand for an object, and in later life it is the basis of literature, theatre, cinema and other creative activities. Just as the child knows that her doll is not a real baby, so adults know that what they are seeing on the cinema screen is not real, but, like the child, they pretend to themselves that it is.

Elements of pretend play

There are three distinct elements in pretend play: the transformation of an object into something else; the giving to an object some make-believe properties; and the invention of imaginary objects.

In the case of the boy flying a pretend plane, the wood in his hand is transformed into metal and acquires the imagined shape of an aircraft; it is endowed with the make-believe property of being able to take off and land; and the pilot flying the plane is totally imaginary.

Using these three elements, a child, even in a severely deprived environment, can indulge in make-believe play. The simplest and crudest of objects can be transformed into something exciting and wonderful. The fact that this pattern of play has been observed all over the world, even in cultures in which it is not encouraged, suggests that it may be an inborn quality of the growing child to develop double-thinking of this kind, making him capable of contemplating possible situations in addition to the actual situation in which he finds himself.

The development of pretend play

As a child moves from age 2 to 5, the complexity of pretend play increases. The 2-year-old already shows signs of wanting to develop solitary pretend play into a more social activity. He usually does this by enlisting a parent or sibling, who has to join in the fantasy by pretending to drink the imaginary tea that the child has just handed over.

By the age of 2½, there is a new development in which substitute objects such as dolls or toy animals, are given feelings of their own. A doll becomes naughty and has to be scolded or a toy animal is tired and must be put to bed. A further extension of this occurs when one of the substitute beings becomes active in its own right and has to control the behaviour of another. One toy animal must try to persuade another one to hide because a monster is coming; or a large doll has to pretend-feed a small doll.

At the age of 3, complementary roles may appear in which a nurse looks after a patient, or a bus driver takes on a new passenger, with parents or siblings roped in to play out the imaginary relationship.

At the age of 4, further complications surface. Now substitute beings start to develop feelings. A doll is sad and lonely, or a toy elephant whose ear has come off is injured and in pain. This type of pretend play reveals that the 4-year-old is already contemplating the moods and feelings of others and is therefore becoming less egocentric.

role play

Role play is a special form of pretend play, in which the child becomes an actor taking on a part and then uses her imagination to perform as if she were someone else. It requires the child to think what it must be like to be someone else and then to act accordingly.

Impersonation and improvisation

Role play does not follow a script. Instead, it involves improvisation and the invention of dramatic interactions between two or more players. The children involved must agree among themselves who will be whom. One will be the doctor and the other the accident victim, or one will be the shopkeeper and the other the shopper. If they tire of their chosen roles they may switch roles and then play on.

All this may look like a simple child's game, but in reality it involves rather complex behaviour on the part of the pre-schoolers. They must be able to mimic the movements, actions and voices of the characters they are impersonating and they must also be able to develop a story line as their shared drama develops. They must trust in one another to support the charade and keep it going.

Imaginary friends

Occasionally, a child engages in a special kind of role play in which she sets up a relationship with an imaginary friend. It may be an invisible presence, or a favourite toy that has been enrolled to play the part of the friend.

Fantasy play

A version of role play involving imaginary friends, especially popular with small boys aged 4 or 5, is that of dressing up as a fictional character, such as Superman or Batman, and behaving as if they are this popular figure. Here, they themselves become the imaginary friend; their own persona disappears and they become someone else. They play out this role relentlessly and over long periods of time, sometimes even insisting on eating and sleeping in their special costumes. Attempts to make them discard it are met with fierce opposition. Inside their heads they are enjoying the extraordinary powers of their fictional hero and his popularity, and find this has an irresistible appeal that they are loath to give up. They may even refuse to answer to their real names, but insist on using those of their adopted characters.

At one time, concern was expressed that a child who behaved in this way, either talking to an invisible friend or dressing up as a fictional character, was experiencing some kind of emotional problem and needed help to overcome her fantasy. This is no longer held to be the case, however, because recent studies have revealed that between 50 and 65 per cent of all pre-school children, at some point, have an imaginary companion or dress up as one. In fact, far from being a problem, this kind of role play is now considered to be an important stepping stone in the development of understanding the feelings, thoughts and beliefs of others.

The advantages of role play

Role play is now seen as an important stage in the mental development of the pre-school child. Because she must invent a dialogue to go with her acted-out dramas, role play helps the development of narrative skills. This aids her in storytelling and the appreciation of storytelling by others. There is also some evidence that role play helps a child to improve her reading and writing skills at a later date. It may also lay the foundations for adult creativity. One famous actor, when asked how he threw himself into one role after another, often with very different personalities, said that it was really very easy – all he had to do was to think back to the days when, as a 4-year-old, he was playing cowboys and Indians and was a cowboy one day and an Indian the next.

collecting and sorting

Between the ages of 4 and 5, there is a strong urge to start classifying the world. A young child learns so much each day, that his brain needs to find a way of organizing new information in order to handle it more easily. This is done by placing things into categories, sorting them into different types and carefully arranging them.

Learning to classify

A first visit to the zoo can be confusing for a 4-year-old. There are so many animals to look at. How can he remember them all? He can help his memory by applying the basic rules of classification. What do all birds have in common – feathers; what do all mammals have in common – fur or hair; what do all reptiles have in common – scales. Then it is down to the next level – lizards have four legs, snakes have none; antelopes have horns, deer have antlers, and so on. As soon as the 4- or 5-year-old has grasped the idea of grouping the zoo animals in this way, he remembers more and more of them. If he sees them simply as a mixed jumble, he finds it much harder.

Forming a collection

Classifying is even more fun if the child can make his own collection of related objects. This may be a collection of toys, such as model cars, bought for him by a parent. He can line them up and arrange and rearrange them, according to size, colour, name, make or some other quality. Again, this allows his brain to develop ways of organizing the elements of life – a mental skill that becomes increasingly important in later years.

Owning a collection of objects that require sorting also introduces the idea of categories and sequences, and of groups and subgroups. It is the starting point of growing an orderly mind that will, in adult life, be able to deal more efficiently with life's complexities.

The ideal collection for a 4-year-old is one that he makes for himself. It can be anything from cards or labels, to shells or flowers, rocks or pebbles. If he himself makes the decisions about which objects to assemble and organize, he not only learns about classifying, but also about finding and owning.

Having personal possessions may become important to the child and the worst crime a parent can commit in such cases is to see his collection as 'rubbish' and throw it away without his consent. A child is capable of bearing a lifelong grudge against a parent for such an act, a resentment that may be out of all proportion to what has happened. This is because the ownership of personal belongings becomes increasingly important as the child approaches school age. His collection is an extension of his personality and to belittle it is to belittle him.

The parent who, instead of scorning the collection, shows an interest in it and asks questions about the various items – which is the best one, why was that one chosen, what is that one called, where did you get than one, which is your favourite – will have a whole new way of interacting with a child, of pleasing him and making him feel important. Better still, a parent can provide a set of shelves or boxes to give the collection a safe place where it will not be disrupted by siblings or visitors.

making and building

One of the great challenges for the pre-school child is to construct something out of raw materials. It starts with a tower of bricks, but soon develops into something much more demanding. Studies show that constructive play is positively linked with intelligence scores.

Building blocks are a versatile and invaluable learning tool for any child, enabling him to explore the different properties of three-dimensional shapes, recognize identical objects by size, shape and colour, and develop visual-spatial skills involving the mental rotation of objects in space. They can also help with learning to count as a child makes the difficult connection between recognizing the sound of a number and linking this to a specific quantity of bricks.

There are assembly kits, craft kits and building kits of many kinds that, with parental help, can occupy a child for many hours. Not every child enjoys this type of play, however. One may take to it immediately and focus all her attention on the sensitive hand skills that are necessary, obtaining huge satisfaction when she sees the finished product materialize in front of her. Another may find it a tedious process and soon lose interest.

Construction kits

Modern construction kits are aimed at developing manual skills and increasing the understanding of simple machinery. There are kits with wheels, gears, levers, axles, hooks, scoops and propellers, all intended to familiarize the 4- or 5-year-old with the basics of engineering and construction. The theory is that playing with such toys also improves the mathematical skills of these children when they are older. A careful study was made to test this theory with a rather surprising result. It was found that the use of construction kits among pre-school children had no effect on their mathematical performances during the early schooldays, but did have a significant impact in their later schooldays. Why there should be this delayed effect is not clear, but it shows that early learning can become deeply embedded in the brain to be utilized much later in life.

It seems likely that, in addition to this proven connection with mathematical skills, the pre-school child who enjoys the mechanics of building things, will also later become a successful builder, architect, engineer or designer.

Imaginative building

Construction materials can also help to stimulate the imagination of the young builder. A simple collection of building bricks can be assembled to make a castle, a palace, a farm or a ship and these imaginary creations can then be peopled with toy soldiers, princes and princesses, farm animals, sailors, and so on. It is easy to buy a ready-made building, but one that has to be built from scratch by the child herself involves a more active stimulation of her mind. It is also more flexible. One day it can be built as a fortress and the next it may be redesigned as a farmhouse.

numbers and counting

In the past, it has sometimes been argued that very young children cannot understand the concept of counting, or of numbers, because they do not yet have the language with which to talk about such things. This view overlooks the fact that apes, and even birds, are capable of counting with remarkable accuracy and they, of course, have no verbal language at all. It seems that there is more to early childhood mathematics than many people have believed.

Counting without numbers

The idea of being able to count without numbers is strange to an adult. But if a bird is offered food in a pot that is covered by a lid marked with a certain number of blobs, and is then offered several pots, all covered by lids, but each marked with a different number of blobs, it will successfully select the one with the original number of blobs on it. The bird does not count, 'one, two, three, four...' as it studies the blobs, because it does not have words for numbers. Instead, it looks at the whole of the lid and, even though the blobs are irregular in shape and varying in size, it is able to assess, in a single overall glance, how many blobs are present. The young child has a similar ability, even before he has learned the one, two, three names for numbers.

Knowledge of these abilities has only been made possible because playgroup organizers have learnt how to introduce informal methods of teaching numeracy to the very young. They have shown that children even as young as 2½ are sometimes capable of nonverbal addition and subtraction. Tests in which black spots are placed on a card and then hidden, after which the child is asked to make a copy of the spots, reveal that they are capable of remembering the numbers involved. In other words, a pre-school child is capable of solving a numbers problem nonverbally before he can solve it verbally, using words for one, two, three, and so on.

This has led some authorities to suggest that the child's brain is programmed to be sensitive to numbers, and that human beings are born with the ability to recognize such features as 'oneness, twoness and threeness'. Toddlers are therefore already primed for the day when verbal counting is added to their knowledge by teaching, and this explains why they can learn to count by numbers so quickly and efficiently.

Mathematical game play

The secret of teaching mathematics to the very young child is to make each test into some sort of game, rather than to apply more formal methods of teaching. Cutting an apple into four equal portions, for example, can be used to demonstrate that two quarters make a half and that two halves make a whole. And sharing out equal numbers of small sweets can also be employed as a way of gradually coming to terms with number differences.

Early on, getting the idea of numbers and the basic concepts of maths, is an easier way to learn than being presented with a set of memorized facts. Once the stage has been reached when numbers do have words – one, two, three – there are many ways in which the fundamental mathematic operations of addition, multiplication and subtraction can be made familiar to a child in a friendly way. The fact that he has ten fingers can be a great help, because he can be shown a parental hand with several fingers hidden from view and then asked to do the same. This makes him check on the number of fingers he is displaying and, little by little, such games as this introduce the concepts of counting and maths as a fun and worthwhile exercise.

attention span

It is sometimes said that the attention span of a young child is only about 3 to 5 minutes. Statements of this kind are, however, highly misleading, as it all depends on what is drawing the child's attention. A 4-year-old may lose interest in playing with a particular toy in less than a minute, but this same child may be prepared to sit down and watch a favourite film for over 2 hours without taking her eyes off the screen once.

Television viewing

With modern children, the television set is sometimes used as a device to give a harassed parent a break. Unfortunately, not all television programmers have an interest in child education and some focus, instead, on capturing a child's attention by rapidly switching from one scene to the next or from one commercial to another. In these instances, the child is given little time to settle on one subject and is bombarded with a nonstop stream of changing images, none of which require long-term concentration. Prolonged exposure to television can therefore encourage the establishment of a short attention span. When the child eventually goes to school and has to face lessons that last for much longer, she finds herself at a disadvantage.

Parental reading

The 4-year-old or 5-year-old child that is fortunate enough to have a parent who is prepared, each day, to sit down with a book and read it carefully and expressively, develops an attention span that gets longer and longer. If it is a good story that captures the young imagination, the period of concentration can last for 20 times longer than the child would manage to sit in front of a television set. A reading once a day sets up an acceptance of extended attention spans. The child is unaware that there is any difference between listening to a story and watching television, but any analysis of the time spent focusing on a single theme shows that, gradually, she is able to stretch her period of concentration. This ability then becomes embedded in her thinking and when she eventually arrives at school she finds the long lessons much easier.

Following feature films

Feature films, surprisingly, are more like books than television, with regard to attention span. They may appear on a screen like TV programmes, but they require a focused concentration for a period of 2 hours rather than 2 minutes. If the film is especially appealing, like one of the children's classics, a small child will sit transfixed through the entire story, and will even do so again a few days later. With each viewing, she remembers a little more of the plot so that, if she then watches it once more, but this time with her parent, she can enjoy the feeling of importance she gets from telling the adult exactly what happens next.

One 4-year-old child who became addicted to the *Star Wars* films was able to explain the difference between a sequel and a prequel to a confused adult. She could name all the characters and understood their complex relationships and their development from film to film.

It could be argued that films like *Star Wars* are of no educational value, being pure fantasy, but this view is mistaken. The precise details are not important here, but rather the fact that the young brain is being made to work hard to learn, name, classify and understand a large cast of characters. It is true that the child will never meet these characters in real life, but her fascination with these films has exercised her brain in the basic processes of naming, classifying and understanding changing relationships. This is generic rather than specific learning, and it prepares the maturing brain cells for categorizing the more practical details that they encounter in the school lessons that come in the years ahead.

the creative child

To be creative is to bring into being something that did not exist before. It is sometimes confused with mimicry and imitative role play (see pages 96–97), but the essence of creativity is that it involves inventing something new. If, for example, a playful adult dances like a bird and asks a child to join in, the result is imitative dancing. If, instead, the adult asks the child to dance like a bird without demonstrating any actions, and the child uses his imagination to transform his arms into wings, and flap them up and down, then he is not mimicking the adult, but being creative.

Measuring creativity

If a child is given a collection of wooden bricks and, without any adult guidance, he spontaneously starts to pile them up, one on top of the other, he is creating a tower. Or perhaps he lines them up along the carpet to create a train. It is always very tempting for an adult to suggest these steps, saying 'let's build a tower' or 'let's make a train' and then demonstrate what to do, followed by the suggestion 'now you try'. It takes some restraint to place a pile of bricks in front of the child and wait to see what happens next. But if this is done, it is possible to watch how the child's imagination sets to work. There is no way of guessing how he will begin to play with the bricks. He might decide to build a wall or make a circle of bricks. Whatever he does without guidance is a measure of his creativity.

Creative disciplines

There are two kinds of creativity: constructive and destructive. The act of creation involves changing the status quo and making something new that was not there before. A child making a tower of bricks without any help can be described as constructive creativity. Destructive creativity is seen when, having made the tower (or having watched a parent make the tower), a child then knocks it down. In both cases, the child alters the existing situation to create something new. In the first case he makes order out of chaos, while in the second he makes chaos out of order. It has to be admitted that acts of destruction have great appeal for the small child. The glee on his face as the pile of bricks comes tumbling down is obvious enough. Toy figures, carefully arranged on the floor in a special way, can be knocked over in the same way with a joyful sweep of the

hand. A sandcastle made on the beach can be squashed flat with one blow. The child relishes the discovery that destructive creativity is so much easier than the constructive kind. A single action creates a massive change in an instant. Bursting a balloon is so much quicker than blowing it up. Negative creativity of this kind, so popular in a harmless way with small children, can become a serious issue if it survives into adulthood.

The young performer

One of the earliest forms of positive creativity in children involves performing – acting, dancing and inventing new games. Even a child as young as 4 years is capable of making up stories and acting them out. Playing on his own, the child may invent an imaginary character with whom he is involved in a drama of his own making. Playing in a group he may invent monsters that chase other children around, pretending to attack them. When there is music, he creates his own dance forms, jumping up and down, bending from side to side, or dashing back and forth in ways that he himself has devised. From a very early age, rhythm is an important element of dancing, and the human brain seems to gain a special reward from activities that involve a regular beat or a rhythmic repetition.

The young artist

Given modelling clay, crayons or paint, the average 4-year-old becomes surprisingly inventive. He starts shaping the clay or making simple images with the crayons and seems to prefer doing so without outside advice. He already has images inside his head and enjoys experimenting with them (see also, Drawing Skills, pages 114–115).

memory and recall

As adults, we find it hard to remember much about the first five years of life. We may be able to recall a few especially exciting moments – or a few really bad ones – but everything else is a blur. This is because, for the very young child, memory is something that is tied to the event that is happening at the moment. Parental teaching can make a big difference in this respect, especially if memory is treated as a form of play.

Learning to remember

Forcing memory skills on to children in a rigid way frequently fails. For the pre-school child, motivation is strongly linked to play and if an activity is fun, he will learn much faster. Nursery rhymes are remembered much more easily than spoken lists, for example.

Some facts have little meaning in the child's world. If, for example, a child is asked what size shoe he is wearing, he is liable to answer 'the same size as my feet' because this makes more sense to him than some abstract numbering system. However, even a useless piece of information like shoe size could be taught to a small child it if were made into a guessing game in a playgroup environment. If everyone has to take his shoes off and is told that the bigger his feet, the bigger the number on his shoes, and he has to guess everyone else's number, the whole business becomes playful and, at the end of the game, the child might well be able to recall the size of his own shoes.

Rehearsal learning

Parents who make up simple remembering games, or spend time singing nursery rhymes and inventing competitions that can only be won if a child can remember certain facts, are helping to programme the young child's brain with memory skills. Even more importantly, by repeating these games over and over again (frequent 'rehearsals'), a parent not only feeds new information into the brain, but also makes the brain more receptive to other new information.

Short-term and long-term memory

A child's brain has a vast capacity for remembering facts – like a sponge soaking up every experience during the day. If every one of these experiences were retained in the memory bank, the brain would quickly become overloaded; with no room for new experiences to be stored. But the brain is also programmed to forget, discarding unimportant facts and keeping useful or impressive ones.

For example, there will be plenty of short-term memories, including what the child ate for supper today, but she may not be able to recall what she ate for supper a week ago. However, she can recall the birthday cake with candles that she was given several months ago. Events associated with exceptional pleasure – or exceptional pain – penetrate deeper and go into the long-term memory bank.

Memory aids

A fact, or an experience, with no powerful emotional content, can only become a long-term memory if it is endlessly repeated (the rehearsal factor), or if a special effort is made to store it. To help a child to remember that she lives at number 5, say, she can use a memory strategy – the number of her house is the same as the number of fingers on one hand. She can also improve her long-term remembering if she organizes her thoughts, creating separate categories for different kinds of facts. And she can make further improvements by asking questions, so that she understands how things work. The better she understands a fact, the easier it is for her to recall it.

Once information has been stored in the long-term memory, it goes on to automatic recall if it is in constant use. Memories that haven't been called on for decades, such as a childhood friend's name, are harder to recover. Unpleasant childhood memories may also be difficult to recall because they have become suppressed. The brain protects itself from them by safely locking them away.

age 4

What's happening inside and out

Brain
At the age of 4, a child's prefrontal cortex (which controls attention, long-term memory and planning functions) is now focused on fine-tuning itself for various tasks.

Teeth
The jaw and facial bones begin to grow and mature, providing the necessary space between the primary teeth for the larger permanent teeth to emerge.

Average weight
Boys: 20 kg (44 lb)   Girls: 12.25 kg (27 lb)

Average height
Boys: 109 cm (43 in)   Girls: 94 cm (37 in)

Head circumference
Boys: 50.4 cm (19¾ in)   Girls: 49.6 cm (19½ in)

Sleep requirements
11–13 hours

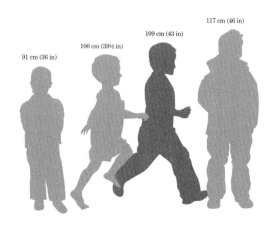

91 cm (36 in)   100 cm (39½ in)   109 cm (43 in)   117 cm (46 in)

the social and emotional world

Organization and responsibility are skills the 5-year-old likes to practise, both at home and at school, and now that she has better control over her emotions, she is more stable in her moods and shows plenty of affection and empathy towards others. Demonstrating newly acquired skills or telling entertaining stories to her friends, is key to the 5-year-old's developing sense of identity. This is mirrored in the fact that she now recognizes herself as an 'agent of action' – where what she does can influence those around her – and who can therefore feel great pride in her accomplishments. However, along with this, the 5-year-old has a newfound ability for self-criticism and may also feel shame when she is made aware that she has done something wrong.

The 5-year-old child is self-assured, likes group activities with highly cooperative play and has plenty of imaginative ideas for games. She now has one or two more-intimate friendships, although she still likes having a wide circle of peer friendships.

In order to develop good relations with their peers, a child needs to be able to recognize social cues from her friends. A child at this age who can control her behaviour in ways that support her friends, will have more successful friendships and avoid rejection.

Why girls like pairs and boys like gangs

At this age, boys and girls tend to diverge in the nature of their friendships. Boys will tend to have a 'gang' of boy friends, while girls form groups of two or three. For a boy, a gang offers the opportunity to determine his hierarchy within a small, controlled circle of boys; a girl is more concerned about her bond with her closest friends, and there can be a lot of competitive jostling among three girl friends to know just who are the two 'best friends' at any one time.

4 the physical world of movement

Mastery of new motor skills are viewed with pride by the 4-year-old, although this increasing self-consciousness may also make him feel inadequate if he sees others mastering a skill he cannot yet do. Skipping on one foot, walking along a straight line and running in circles are new skills that the 4-year-old will start practising over and over again in any number of playground games. By the time a child has turned 4, he will almost certainly have developed a consistent preference for using his left or right hand, and this specialization of fine motor skills sees a steady development in the ability to write letters and draw shapes, as well as skill at hitting objects accurately with a hammer.

The developing ability to balance makes climbing up trees and ladders and jumping over objects a feasible challenge now, and, as balance improves, so too does the 4-year-old's desire to try out wheeled toys, such as scooters and bikes.

Many traditional playground games are the perfect way for children to refine their gross motor skills. Hopscotch requires a child to mix up a combination of hopping (on alternate legs) and jumping as well as turning – all perfect for practising balance.

Why sleep is good for boys

Research has shown a link between a lack of sleep and hyperactivity, although it is not clear whether the hyperactivity causes a lack of sleep, or whether children with short or fragmented sleep patterns are then sleepy during the day, which paradoxically prompts hyperactivity in boys. However, as long as a 4-year-old was achieving a relatively stable 11 hours of sleep each night, he was much less likely to be hyperactive.

At this age, a child will commonly draw people as a large head with stick legs and arms. This could be due to the importance a child gives to people's faces, while the rest of the body is considered less crucial for the overall picture. However, it is also believed that this might be because the child's working memory only allows for so much information at one time.

Around the age of 5, a child can clearly distinguish categories called 'class inclusion' (also known as set theory), where she will realize that if there's a class of food called fruit in the supermarket and that apples are a subset of fruit, then there will be apples in the supermarket, along with other subsets of fruit, such as pears, plums and pineapples. These are newly developed and more complex levels of hierarchical reasoning than a child has been aware of before this age.

Reading at 5

While most schools encourage children to start reading at the age of 5, recent research suggests that this is unlikely to improve a child's long-term reading skills. Children in the study who had learnt to read early (from age 5) and those who had learnt late (from 7) were equally matched in reading abilities by the age of 11. Instead it is thought that the factors affecting long-term reading abilities are language and learning skills that a child picks up through informal play. It is also believed that language development overall is a better indicator of long-term reading skills than any formal ability at reading.

language and learning

The 4-year-old is a dramatic and imaginative storyteller. Her vocabulary now contains over 1,500 words and she likes to play with similar sounding words. Using long, complete sentences, a child at 4 will also change her tone of voice to adapt to her listener's level of understanding, so she may use a baby voice when talking to a toddler, and a grown-up voice for talking with adults. She fluently uses prepositions to describe the location of things, as well as a range of possessive pronouns – his, hers, theirs, Mummy's – and adds -ed to the ends of words (although often mistakenly; 'I bikeded down the street'). A firmer grasp of a daily sequence of events as well as object permanence means that the 4-year-old can now easily relate to people or objects that are not currently present. She will also be able to recognize and name up to eight colours, and likes to 'read' books, although the story may be more about her imagination than the words on the page.

Mimicry is at its peak at this age, and the 4-year-old will now enthusiastically try anything new – as long as she sees a trusted adult trying it too. She will relish playing at job roles – a nurse, a fireman, a teacher, perhaps – and this kind of play also helps this age group work through fears and fantasies.

language and learning

By the age of 5, a child has a very clear understanding of the structure of time – days, weeks, months and even years – and can make sense of a calendar. However, he may still struggle with the notion of having to wait a month (or even a day) for something he really wants. He now asks not only what something is called but also what it means and how it fits within its context. This search for meaning extends to most areas of a 5-year-old's life, and is linked to the fact that he now understands that words have a metaphorical meaning as well as a concrete meaning. A 5-year-old understands the concepts of tallest, smallest, largest, shortest and can arrange them into serial positions: from the first to the last, the smallest to the largest. Now counting up to 100, a child also understands what half means, although he may struggle with other fractions. The child at 5 has also developed a clear sense of right and wrong as well as what he believes to be fair and true.

By now, a child can recognize and probably write his own name, and his 2,000-or-so word vocabularly allows him a wider opportunity for joke- and story-telling.

Being able to communicate is perhaps the most important skill when it comes to a child's success at play at this age – research demonstrates that pre-schoolers who speak clearly and who can communicate their ideas more effectively, tend to have longer periods of play with other children.

Recognizing false beliefs

At the age of 4, a child can understand that another person's perspective on a situation may be different from his own and then predict their behaviour. Numerous studies have shown that up until the age of 4, most children cannot grasp this concept, which is also known as the false-belief theory. To demonstrate this, researchers show a child two dolls in a room where there is a basket and a box. One of the dolls places a marble in the basket, then leaves the room; while she's gone, the other doll takes the marble out of the basket and puts it into the box. When the first doll returns, the child is asked where the first doll will look for the marble. If the child answers that the first doll will look in the basket, she will have grasped the concept of false belief.

5-year-olds should be encouraged to be as active as possible, as the benefits of this activity can be 'banked' for years to come. Researchers looked at children at the ages of 5, 8 and then 11, and discovered that the most active children at 5 had less fat at both 8 and 11, even if their exercise levels had decreased at these later ages.

The concept of body image

A study of 2- to 6-year-old girls, carried out by the University of Central Florida, has shown that one-third would like to change at least one physical attribute such as weight or hair colour; nearly half say they worry about being fat. According to the research, the criticism and teasing received from parents, siblings and peers is the main reason for this.

Various studies have shown that a child who follows a music programme for at least three years around the age of 5, will have more advanced locomotor skills (running, hopping, skipping, sliding), fine motor skills (in both hands), as well as motor-sequencing abilities, language skills and IQ than children who do not.

the physical world of movement

Able to dress herself – generally without any help – and even perhaps tying her own shoelaces, the 5-year-old child is now much more independent. She is now printing simple letters and is almost always consistent with the hand she uses for drawing, writing and cutting. She can turn somersaults and construct three-dimensional objects with her building blocks. Whether it is dancing, jumping a skipping rope, playing a musical instrument, doing puzzles, throwing and catching balls, swimming or riding a bicycle, a mix of activities is the ideal way for the 5-year-old to develop her gross and fine motor skills to their optimum.

The 4-year-old has good balance and may even be able to skate and ride a two-wheeler bicycle. Able to jump forwards up to 10 times in a row without falling over, she can also walk backwards heel to toe.

the social and emotional world

4

There is an element of defiance in the 4-year-old as he tests himself and others against newly learnt conventions, but he will also show pride in his accomplishments and seek out approval from adults. Friendships take on greater significance for the 4-year-old, and he will usually have a circle of many friends with one or two best friends. Along with real friends, more than half of 4-year-olds will have an imaginary playmate. There are mood swings at this age too, and frequently the well-mannered 4-year-old will throw things in a fit of frustration. Now, however, these fits will be followed by a sense of regret, as the 4-year-old understands the consequences of his actions.

Talkative and sure of himself, the 4-year-old is now an expert at cooperative play and has discovered the joy of games that use simple rules: hide and seek, tag, Simon says.

There are many different strategies the 4-year-old will use when faced with conflict with a peer, but research shows that if the conflict is with an acquaintance, the child tends to simply stop playing with the other child. However, when the conflict is with a close friend, the child will use negotiation, compromise and conciliatory gestures to try to resolve the dispute.

Recognizing difference

As he recognizes the difference between the self and the other at around the age of 3, a child will begin to consciously categorize the world around him. His awareness of this difference peaks at the age of 4, when he may point out differences of skin colour, age, disability and, of course, gender. While this can lead to some embarrassingly frank statements from a 4-year-old, research suggests that discussing the difference quite openly (although perhaps not in public) is the best way to help a child at this age to create positive relationships with the person whom he sees as different to himself.

age 5

What's happening inside and out

Brain
By the age of 5, a child's brain is 90 per cent of its adult size. It is continuing to make significant synaptic developments, where neurons are connecting to one another, creating a huge network of pathways.

Teeth
A 5-year-old may get a 'wobbly' tooth because a secondary 'adult' tooth is coming through.

Average weight
Boys: 22.5 kg (50 lb)   Girls: 14 kg (31 lb)

Average height
Boys: 117 cm (46 in)   Girls: 101 cm (40 in)

Head circumference
No longer measured

Sleep requirements
10–11 hours

81 cm (32 in)   88 cm (34½ in)   94 cm (37 in)   101 cm (40 in)

the amazing world of fours and fives

Self-assured and talkative, the child is now a confident and imaginative individual who is testing himself against the social rules his world offers him. However, he now has a sense of consequence and recognizes that his behaviour has an impact on others. With a year or two of socializing behind him, he has many friendships with a wide circle of peers, but he also has a few close friends, and perhaps one or two imaginary friends. Being a boy or a girl takes on a new significance as the 4-year-old starts to relate with others of the same gender and enjoys role-playing. With a firmer sense of who they are in the world, at the end of these years the child will be highly capable and willing to express their own thoughts on life, the universe and everything.

≪ the child at 4

the child at 5 ≫

drawing skills

Between the ages of 2 and 5, every child that has access to pencil and paper will undertake an exciting journey from random scribbling to lively picture-making. Amazingly, the visual stages through which all children pass are much the same regardless of where they live. Only after the age of 5 do local influences start to play a role.

Early scribbles

Any 2-year-old who is given a pencil and paper will start to make what appear to be random scribbles. These lines, going repeatedly back and forth, up and down or round and round, seem no more than records of arm movements. But they quickly become more than that because, if the pencil point breaks and stops making marks, the child gives up. The reward comes not from the movement alone, but from its visual impact. As the months pass, the child begins to vary the scribbles, trying zigzags, circles or meandering lines. Twenty different scribble-types have been identified.

The first diagrams

The 3-year-old tires of multi-scribbles and attempts to create some order. She begins to simplify her lines. Clumsy, circling scribbles become circles; crisscrosses become vertical crosses, diagonal crosses, triangles or squares; and irregular scribble patterns are reduced to amoebic shapes.

The 3-year-old now starts to play with these six basic diagrams, adding one to another. If a triangle is put on top of a square it gives her the basis for a house. If small circles are put inside a big circle she discovers a pattern that eventually becomes a face. These linked diagrams are called 'combines'. The next stage is to put several combines together, making 'aggregates'. There are countless possibilities now, and, if children are left to their own devices, a few become favoured over all others and will form the basis for making the first recognizable, pictorial images when the child reaches 4 years.

The first true images

On reaching her fourth birthday, the budding artist starts to create delightfully primitive human figures. The simplest ones have a big round face, which is also the body. Lines often radiate from this face-body – two below for legs, two more at the sides for arms and smaller ones above for hair. The eyes, nose and mouth are usually little more than spots. Other details tend to be omitted altogether. Almost every child in the world makes a version of this figure – the 'cephalopod' – providing he has been left to invent his own shapes.

As the months pass, the 4-year-old artist tries to improve on this figure. A body is formed by drawing a horizontal line between the legs. Unfortunately this leaves the arms coming out of the sides of the head, and it takes some time before they are lowered. Blobs at the ends of the arms and legs become hands and feet, and fingers may be added. On the face, the eyes may sprout eyelashes and the open mouth may gain teeth. Little by little the child is building on its basic shapes, making them more and more complex.

Primitive compositions

By the age of 5, the artist has started to compose whole scenes, such as placing human figures next to a house, some flowers, a dog and a car. All these elements are fashioned in a charmingly simple way, with the whole composition full of rhythm and verve. This is the peak age for child art, when the brain has reached a stage of creativity that reflects very clearly what is going on inside the artist's imagination. She includes everything that is important, while excluding anything that is unimportant.

The images of the happy child are, by now, markedly different from those of the sad child, and the drawings of the 5-year-old artist can tell us a great deal about their developing personality. If we read them correctly, these drawings tell us much more about the way a child's brain is maturing than any verbal conversation. Sadly, when the 6-year-old goes to school, she soon loses the raw creativity that made her early pictures so appealing.

pre-writing

Although all children, given free access to pencil and paper, show a natural tendency to make scribbles that slowly develop into drawings without parental guidance, the development of writing needs special help. The distillation of the letters of the alphabet from the early scribbling requires considerable assistance, because there is nothing natural about alphabets or scripts. Each culture has its own version of writing and an Arab child, a Russian child and an English child all have to learn a very different set of writing units.

From scribbling to pre-writing

The 3-year-old who is at the stage of multiple scribbling is often fascinated to see parents writing notes in longhand. Because he can tell that these notes are important, he may try to mimic them by doing his own version of writing. He modifies his exploratory, multiple scribbles into more restrained lines of smaller scribbles that he announces proudly are written messages. After a while, he breaks the lines of scribbles up into short lengths in an attempt to imitate separate words. This scribble-writing with its scribble-words is completely undecipherable. The pre-writer may be proud of the way he has copied adult writing and should be praised for his efforts, but this very early stage has to be tamed by adult teaching before true writing can occur.

From pre-writing to writing

In his drawings, the 3-year-old child starts to simplify his multiple scribblings and makes more distinct shapes such as circles, crosses and zigzags (see pages 114–115). Out of these shapes, without much help, he gradually starts to make his first, simple pictorial images. It is from this process that parents or teachers can, so to speak, hijack the natural shape-play and divert it into creating the units of the alphabet. A circle becomes the letter O; a half-circle becomes a D; a short vertical line becomes an I; a zigzag becomes a W or a Z, and so on. By the age of 4 more angles are evident in a child's scribble and his ability to copy geometric forms shows his readiness to start learning to write. If the inquisitive child is shown a whole alphabet written out on a page and is asked to copy it, letter by letter, he will, at some stage, find this an exciting challenge. When he makes his own ABCDEF... underneath the elegant adult version he is frustrated at first, because his letters are clumsy by comparison, but this drives him on to repeat them over and over again until he has improved them.

From letters into words

The next step is for the child to group his crudely formed letters together into words – the start of his long journey towards proper writing. At first, he attempts this without any stable baseline and his letters are scattered all over the page. Some may be drawn backwards or on their sides, but gradually they get themselves into the proper configuration and become grouped in a more organized manner.

The child then finds that letters made up of only vertical and horizontal lines, such as T, I, L or H, are easier to create than those with more complicated elements. Letters that combine straight and curved lines, such as B, G or P, or letters with diagonal lines, such as N, K or Y, are harder.

Words created by a 5-year-old are often hard to interpret. MAKI, ORIJUS and MOHROM may not mean much to an adult, but to the child they are part of a shopping list and stand for MILK, ORANGE JUICE and MUSHROOM.

The typical 5-year-old is usually capable of writing his first name clearly in simple capital letters. The individual letters may be a little shaky and poorly arranged on the paper, but he has at least achieved the moment of identifying himself with his very first signature. This is the stage his writing will have reached by the time he leaves the pre-school phase behind him. In his early schooldays he will start to make massive strides in his writing ability and, in a few years, he will be producing handwriting that is legible.

the emotional journey

toddler frustration

At what age is a human being at her most aggressive? Does a peak of violence show itself most strongly among unruly teenagers? Or perhaps among disgruntled middle-aged individuals who feel that they have been badly treated by life? Surprisingly, the answer is that the most violent age of all occurs when the toddler reaches the age of 2.

The terrible twos

We often hear about the rages and temper tantrums of the 2-year-old and how, at this tender age, children develop an antisocial temperament that has been the cause of much debate. Some parents refuse to accept this, denying any evidence of it in their own, much loved 2-year-olds. There are, of course, exceptions to every rule, but if we are to believe the results obtained by a painstaking, objective analysis of the conduct of toddlers in a playgroup, we are forced to accept the fact that 'the terrible twos' is not, after all, a misnomer.

Long-term research, involving thousands of subjects, has revealed that an average 2-year-old child who spends an hour playing with other children of the same age, performs one physically aggressive act for every four social interactions. Compared with the typically peaceful interactions that we expect to see among human adults in social situations, this is alarmingly high.

The biggest problem facing the 2-year-old is that, in terms of development, her brain is slightly ahead of her body. She develops ambitions to perform actions that her body finds it hard to complete. Her limb movements and manipulations are still rather clumsy and it takes some months for her to refine them, but she keeps on trying and when she fails, it makes her angry.

This anger may grow into a full-blown temper tantrum if parents try to intervene. If they feel her anger needs disciplining, they only make matters worse. What the frustrated child needs is comfort and encouragement, not rebuke. Her emotional outburst may make this difficult, but if it can be managed this may work wonders, especially if it helps her to beat the challenge she has set herself.

Self-comforting actions

If frustrations are not overcome they can easily leave the 2-year-old in a state of conflict. If these feelings become intense, the toddler may start performing various self-comforting actions. These appear to be little more than meaningless tics, but in reality they allow the frustrated individual to find an outlet for her blocked urges. Any action, no matter how irrelevant, is better than no action at all.

Some self-comforting actions take the form of regressing to infancy. The frustrated 2-year-old may suck her thumb, or, if it is long enough, suck her hair or rock her body back and forth. The thumb-sucking takes her back to the warm comforts of sucking at her mother's breast and the back-and-forth rocking of her body recreates the maternal rocking used to soothe her with when she was a tiny baby finding it hard to get to sleep.

Other frustration responses have a destructive element. These take the form of attacks aimed at the child's own body, almost as if she is punishing herself for failing in a task she has set herself. She may start biting her nails, rubbing her nose, or pulling at her hair.

Because these actions act as a minor distraction from the frustration the toddler has experienced, they provide a brief reward. This can lead to trouble because the rewarding sensation gained from them may mean that they are repeated time and again even when the frustration has passed. There is then the risk that they may become fixed habits that are hard to break. If there is the slightest tension, the thumb goes to the mouth and the thumb is sucked. If there is a mild feeling of unhappiness, the nails are bitten again and again, until eventually they are right down to the quick. Repeated hair sucking can lead to the creation of a hairball of the kind better known in cats than humans. And aggressive hair pulling can result in the child making herself partially bald. In all these cases great sympathy is needed and parental ingenuity is required to find ways of reducing and, in the course of time, eliminating these unfortunate habits.

Improving relationships

Socially, the 2-year-old is concerned mostly with himself, but by the age of 5 he is able to interact in a friendly way with others of his age and understands the concepts of both competition and cooperation. The rapid development of language during this period enables him to communicate his feelings to his friends and to accept the need to share and take turns in group activities. He still tries to get his own way, but understands that this does not always happen and discovers that it is sometimes more comfortable to follow than to lead.

emotional strength

During the past forty years, there has been a major shift in childcare during the pre-school years as more and more women have gone out to work, so giving rise to the need for day care. The pre-school child has had to learn to cope with separation and forming new social attachments with carers and other members of their day care group. The type of care has an impact on their social and emotional growth.

Home care or playgroup?

Today the majority of young children – 64 per cent of 3- and 4-year-olds – are experiencing what is called 'early years education'. The reason is simple. In earlier times almost all mothers spent the first 5 pre-school years with their children. But as the decades have passed, many mothers have returned to work earlier and had to find a suitable childcare solution.

Socially speaking there are three types of pre-schoolers:
The stay-at-home children: those who spend all their time with their mothers.
The away-day children: those who spend their days away from home with nannies and child minders, and other children of the same age.
The home-and-away children: those who enjoy the best of both worlds – spending a great deal of time with their mothers, but also occasionally spending time in a childcare situation with other children.

The stay-at-homes benefit from more prolonged interaction with loving parents. These interactions are intensive and result in greater advances in learning and intelligence. The away-days enjoy far less of this one-to-one intimacy but benefit from greater exposure to social encounters and group activities. Those who enjoy the best of both these worlds develop both high intelligence and high sociability.

Recent studies suggest that the children of working mothers, placed in nursery schools for long periods of time, are slightly more backward and slightly more assertive when they eventually reach school age. What they have gained in social skills they have lost in levels of learning. With good schooling, however, they soon catch up.

Bonding and attachment

During the first 5 years of life, a child is genetically programmed to attach himself emotionally to a primary care-giver. In the majority of cases this carer is the biological mother, but in her unavoidable absence it may be someone else. In addition to the primary carer, there may be several other significant carers, such as fathers, grandmothers, older sisters or nannies. It was originally thought that the attachment was based on 'cupboard love', in other words the child attached himself emotionally to the person who gave him food, drink and protection, but this has proved not to be the case. Attachment goes deeper than this and is based purely on feelings of safety and security, these feelings having been obtained by prolonged physical contact involving a great deal of contact-intimacy such as cuddling, hugging and soft embraces.

When the ideas about attachment were first introduced in the middle of the 20th century, it was found that a nursery school that had strong links to the parents of its children had greater success in dealing with problems of temporary separation. If the school carers knew the mothers of the children well, it became easier for them to become trusted support-carers. The children came to trust them and developed secondary attachments to them.

The young child is capable of coping with several close attachments, both at home with his primary care-givers and with secondary carers in a childcare situation, just so long as they all involve the feeling of safety and security, in addition to the more practical rewards of food and drink. Wherever a tiny child finds himself, he must have at least one adult available to whom he can run for a comforting hug or a cuddle when he is frightened or hurt.

the flexible face

Interpreting a child's facial expresssions is key to understanding her emotions. Studies show that less than 10 per cent of feelings are expressed in words, whereas more than 90 per cent are expressed nonverbally. As a child develops mentally and physically, the range and complexity of her facial and other visual signs increases, as does her ability to manipulate it.

Pulling faces

One of the great discoveries made by the child as she progresses from 2 to 5 years is the amazing flexibility of her face. She starts out with simple smiles, pouts and frowns and then realizes that she can play with these expressions and even invent new ones for fun, revelling in the comic effect they have and the reactions of those around her. The result, by the age of 4 and 5, is that there is an increasing amount of face-pulling and every parent knows how difficult it is to obtain a good photograph for the family album without a tiny face insisting on putting on a silly grimace from their vast repertoire for the camera.

The human being has the most highly developed set of facial muscles in the entire animal kingdom. Even the expressive chimpanzee cannot match the range and subtlety of human facial signals. All over the world these signals are the same and it is usually easy to tell the precise mood of a small child by the look she is giving you. All the emotions – fear, disgust, sadness, surprise, anger and happiness – are written there. The pre-school child is only just beginning to learn the adult skill of hiding emotions from others. Even the silly expressions, when she is deliberately face-pulling, are a signal of her mood – one of show-off playfulness.

body language

Apart from facial expressions, a child's body sends out two kinds of visual signal. These are the general body postures and movements – the crouched body, the slumped body, the erect body, and so on – and the conscious gestures and unconscious gesticulations of the arms and hands. Both are expressive of mood and feelings.

Hand gestures

Adults make two kinds of hand gesture. They move their hands about when trying to emphasize the words they are speaking. These gesticulations are not planned, but done unconsciously, and they do not occur when the person is silent. Adults may also use deliberate, symbolic gestures, in which the hand action replaces speech. The small child rarely uses such signals. He may clench his fists when he is angry and make a few other simple gesticulations, but he lacks the refinement and complexity of the adult. With symbolic gestures, from an early age, a child waves his hands as a greeting or a farewell, and will also use his hands to point in a direction, but beyond that there are few attempts to make a symbolic hand sign.

Body postures

What he lacks in subtle hand movements, the small child makes up for with his body postures. He shows his delight by jumping wildly up and down on the spot, and he signals his boredom with a dramatically slumped body and shuffling feet. Frustration may be shown by a rhythmic swinging of the body from side to side; anger by stamping his feet on the ground.

Development of body language

There are two sides to body language – sending signals and receiving them. Tests have shown that, with pre-school children, the understanding of the expressions and gestures of others precedes the making of these signals by the child himself. In other words, comprehension precedes production. And the development of facial skills precedes gestural skills. Other tests have revealed that a child's popularity is greater when his nonverbal skills are better. To put it another way, a child is more liked by his young friends if he is more visually expressive.

In one experiment in which children were observed while watching films, it emerged that they make more facial expressions when they are watching with a friend than when they are watching alone. Also girls make more expressions than boys. This means that they are already making faces to share their moods with others, and that boys, even at this tender age, have started to suppress their outward feelings more than girls.

the clingy child

A child who is not readily sociable is one of three types: she may be a loner who prefers her own company to that of others; she may be a shy child who wishes to be sociable but is too timid to interact freely with others (see pages 130–131); or she may be a clingy child who cannot bear to be parted from her adult protector, usually her mother.

The fear of independence

The behaviour of the clingy child is essentially infantile. It is appropriate for a baby to be close to her mother. She is physically helpless and dependent on her for everything. But as she grows and becomes more active, her pleasure at becoming more independent increases with each year. As a 2-year-old she plays with other children of her own age, while keeping an eye on her mother to make sure she is still nearby. By the age of 3 she is prepared to play with other children for a while, even in the absence of her mother. By 4 or 5, she is prepared to spend a longer time away from her primary protector, at a playgroup or at parties with other children. By contrast, the clingy child is much slower in taking these first steps towards independent action and struggles to move beyond the 2-year-old stage, where she cannot bear to lose sight of her mother.

It is important to realize that separation anxiety is perfectly natural among very young children. The mother, or main carer, is the most important person in the life of the child and it is understandable that the child is suspicious of strangers and does not want to be cut off from the one person that she fully trusts. Working against this feeling is her urge to explore and to become a free agent. The balance between these two conflicting urges, to cling and to explore, gradually shifts as time goes on, but for some children this shift is much slower than usual.

Making the break

There are several ways in which to help a clingy child. Paradoxically, the child that wants to cling too much should be given extra hugs and cuddles. Any attempt to push her away only increases her desire to stay put. The more at ease and secure she feels, the more she will be prepared to risk exploring the world beyond her mother.

Secondly, the clinger should be reassured that any separations will be very short. This can be confirmed by setting up some separations that, as promised, only last a few minutes. Once the child comes to trust the promise that the protector will soon return, she is ready for a slightly longer separation. In this way, little by little, the panic at being left alone is reduced. One of the problems for a child in these cases is that she starts to sense the anxiety that she herself causes her parent. The loving mother hates to see her child unhappy when being left at a party or a playgroup, and finds it hard to hide her emotions. Sneaking away when the child is not looking can cause a massive panic. It is far better to say a quick, cheerful goodbye and explain that she will be back very soon – then leave without further delay.

The cause of separation-anxiety

One of the reasons for a child becoming excessively clingy is that she has not been made to feel secure enough at home. The child of the overtly loving mother, who praises her child, often hugs and reassures her, will find her more prepared to explore the world than the mother who is less expressive. The colder, more off-hand mother makes the child feel insecure and it is this sense of insecurity that makes the child fearful of losing what little she has.

A child can also be made more clingy because of some specific, unpleasant event that occurs during one of her first outings. If she is left at a party or in a playgroup when she is very young and one of the other children there hurts her or frightens her in some way, this can easily cause a serious setback in increasing the child's independence.

the shy child

Shyness in a child is often misunderstood. A boy who is timid, withdrawn and rather quiet is sometimes viewed as antisocial. Because he chooses to play on his own, it is assumed that he doesn't want to play with others and that he is a loner. But if his behaviour is the result of shyness, this is not the case. If he is shy, he wants to play with others, but is reluctant to do so. He is not a loner, but a sociable child who, for some reason, finds it unusually hard to make friends and interact with other children. The true loner enjoys being on his own, but the shy child does not and it is important to make a distinction between the two.

Home and away

At home, shyness is not usually a serious problem and comes to the surface far less than when the child is away from home. It begins to make an impact when the child attends a party and finds that the idea of joining in the fun is frightening, even when his parent is present. The instinct worsens at nursery, where the protective parent is absent.

One of the characteristics of shyness is that it is strongly resistant to adult criticism. If an embarrassed parent tries to push a shy child into being more sociable, the result is usually to make matters much worse. Saying 'Don't be silly, everyone else is doing it' is almost certain to intensify the feeling of shyness. It makes the child who is already unhappy about his inability to join in, feel like a misfit who is being singled out. This only magnifies his anxiety and the social event he is attending is marked down in his memory as something to be avoided at all costs.

Joining a group

Any child showing severe shyness when first attending a playgroup can be helped in several ways. A sensitive teacher knows that she must not push or hurry such a child and watches carefully to see how he behaves as time goes on. Introducing nonverbal sharing games such as bouncing a ball back and forth from child to child, enables the shy child to take part with minimal verbal interaction.

If one of the other children in the group approaches the shy child and sits with him, a friendship on a one-to-one basis may be established, even if group interaction is still difficult. Having this one special friend can be an important first step towards socializing the shy child. The watchful teacher can then 'accidentally' arrange for the shy child to be paired with his one special friend in some group game, and the special friend now becomes the bridge that can lead to full integration with the others. If it can be arranged for this special playmate to visit the shy child at home, where they play together and strengthen their bond of attachment, this can also help in the process of defeating the shyness.

Parents often worry unnecessarily about shyness in their child, when all that is needed is patience and avoiding any kind of bullying or criticism. If the child is allowed to take his time in adjusting to social activities, he will get there eventually. It is a comfort to know that a quiet, thoughtful pre-school child may, in adult life, end up as a greater success than many of the high-spirited, outgoing members of his playgroup. It takes all kinds to make up adult society and the ex-shy child may have special roles to play that do not suit the personality of the ex-boisterous child.

The cause of shyness

It is worth asking what makes a particular child unusually shy. A careful study carried out with children who had been classified as such, revealed that there were special circumstances in their home life that were significant. It was discovered that, at home, shy children spoke less than non-shy children and, interestingly, the parents of shy children spoke less than the parents of non-shy children and were generally more aloof. The fun-and-games parents, who talked a lot to their children and interacted with them frequently in a loving and friendly way, rarely had children who were shy in company.

confidence

When children arrive for their first day at a playgroup, some are nervous and anxious and others are excited and confident. What is it about the background of these children that separates them into these two types? And what can parents do to encourage the timid ones to be more self-confident?

Differences from birth

Partly, these differences in personality are in a child's genes. Any parent with several children will know that, from birth, there can be striking differences in personality. One child is an extrovert, always lively and ready to enjoy anything that life has to offer. Another will be reserved and much quieter. And another may be a bundle of nerves whenever her routine is broken. Even if the children are all treated exactly the same by loving parents, these differences may persist and last a lifetime. Sensitive parents, spotting these differences early on, can do their best to prevent the extroverts from becoming too bumptious and to boost the confidence of the others.

Overconfidence

The child who is overconfident already has a high opinion of herself and this self-esteem carries her a long way. If, however, she feels that she can do everything better than other children, she may find herself becoming unpopular. In most cases, it is simple enough to get her to see that if she holds back a little, the other children will warm to her. She will be hurt if her confidence is punished, but will understand if it is explained to her gently that it is helpful to think of the other children's feelings.

Lack of confidence

The child that lacks confidence is more difficult to help. She may have inherited a quieter personality, but a large part of her problem is probably the way she has been treated by her family. There are several ways that her self-esteem may have suffered needlessly. The most common problem stems from the manner in which she is praised or criticized for how she behaves from day to day. All too often a child is severely criticized when she does something wrong but is only mildly praised (if at all) for doing

something right. This quickly undermines self-esteem and is much more common than most people realize. It is thoughtless rather than malicious. An old brother or sister may be quick to criticize, but may rarely have a good word to say. A harassed parent may be ready to scold every fault, but does not take the time to heap praise on something well done. Scolding should be reserved solely for occasions when a child seriously deserves it. Even then, with a shy child, it should be muted rather than strident.

Some parents like to appear infallible to their small child and are reluctant to apologize when they have made a mistake, finding some excuse for themselves. If a simple, honest apology is made when they have been at fault the child will appreciate this more than most parents realize.

An introverted child may embarrass a parent in a social situation, especially where other children are happily uninhibited. In such instances, there is a strong temptation to apologise for the child, which she overhears. This only makes matters worse, as the child badly needs to know that her parent is proud of her and tells this to other people.

Some parents respond to a child's lack of confidence by fussing over her. For example, at a stage where the child can easily dress herself, the parent insists on doing it for her. This makes her feel useless and, if done in a public place, can cause acute embarrassment. Encouraging her to do things for herself helps to boost his self-esteem.

These points may seem obvious, but they are faults that occur with amazing frequency. In most instances, with a little extra thought, they can so easily be corrected, giving the quiet child's self-confidence a massive boost that will see her trot off to her playgroup with her head held high.

emotional intelligence

Emotional intelligence has nothing to do with intellect. It has, instead, to do with understanding one's own emotions and those of others, and knowing how to handle them. A child with a high IQ is not necessarily good at this. He may be able to solve puzzles easily, but when it comes to making friends, he may lack the necessary social skills, and may find that children who are less clever are nevertheless more popular.

Reading other children

If two new boys join a playgroup, one may make friends much more quickly than the other. He succeeds because he can intuitively read the emotions of the others and can tell which ones are more likely to be responsive. He also has better control over his own emotions. The boy who fails to make friends may be very bright intellectually, but he ignores the moods and feelings of other members of the group and, as a result, encounters more resistance.

Improving emotional intelligence

As a child's sense of self develops, so does his awareness of other people vis-à-vis himself. Emotional awareness starts with primary emotions such as happiness, fear, sadness, anger and surprise, followed by secondary emotions such as pride, guilt, shame and embarrassment. Pre-school children are not too young to develop true emotional intelligence. It requires nurturing and there are several ways in which this can be done. If someone is sad, the child can be asked to help cheer her up. In this way, the emotions of others can gradually become better understood. One simple game is to ask the child to draw faces showing different emotions: sad, angry, happy, surprised and frightened. This can lead to a discussion of how one can tell the mood of other people. An alternative is to play an acting game in which the child has to pretend to be sad, angry, happy, and so on.

Controlling the emotions

One way to measure emotional control is the famous 'marshmallow' test. In this test a single marshmallow is put on a plate and placed on a table. The child is told that he can eat it now if he wants to, but that, if he waits until the adult returns, he can have five marshmallows. The adult then leaves the room. In one case, the child simply grabs the marshmallow and eats it. Another holds out for a few minutes before eating it. A third child does everything he can to distract himself from thoughts of the marshmallow and then, when the adult returns, he gets his reward.

This third child displays 'impulse control' – a control over his emotions that, in more serious circumstances, enables him to deal efficiently with difficult social conflicts. It is claimed that a 4-year-old child's performance in this test is a better indicator of how he will succeed in later life than any IQ test. This is because delayed gratification is one of the most important factors in the way we handle our adult emotional lives.

An interesting question is at what age do children develop emotional deception? Some researchers have suggested that children as young as 3 years are able to hide their emotions or deliberately manipulate their facial expressions to deceive other people, while other psychologists believe that this only happens at around 4 or 5 years old.

Sharing emotions

For some reason, parents tend to think of emotional problems as essentially part of the adult world and take little trouble to discuss emotions with small children. It does not occur to a mother to describe to her child how she, as a parent, is feeling at any given moment. If something good has happened and the mother is brimming with good humour, it only takes a few moments to explain this. If she has had a bad day, again she can sit down and discuss with the child what has upset her. The more the child learns about the moods of others, the better able he will be to deal with social problems of his own.

empathy and kindness

The 2-year-old is self-centred, because she has only just become able to explore the world around her. During the next few years the developing child begins to think more about other people and starts to display acts of kindness. There are two main sources of this kindness – on the one hand, there is a natural urge of human beings to cooperate with one another and, on the other, a desire to imitate parental behaviour.

The inborn urge to cooperate

It has been said in the past that mankind is essentially wicked and must be made good by instruction and the imposition of a moral code. In the doctrine of original sin there is no place for inborn human kindness or cooperation. We are born as savage animals and can only be made good by the church's teaching. This view has lasted for centuries and the implication is that a tiny child is a bundle of selfish, violent greed and can only be tamed by wise adult training.

Nothing could be further from the truth: humans could not have evolved that way. When our ancient ancestors came down from the trees and became hunter-gatherers they could not have survived without a newfound urge actively to help one another. In order to thrive, man had to evolve this inborn urge to cooperate, balancing it against the more ancient urge to compete with one another. Unless we developed a balance between these two drives – helping and competing – we would never have enjoyed the evolutionary success that allowed us to conquer the world.

The helpful child

The urge to be kind and helpful to one another starts to show itself in the very young child at around the age of 4 and 5. She is already intelligent enough to know that, if she is given a group task, she will fail – unless she cooperates. The competitive urge is still present, and there may be some argument as to who will be in charge of the group in order to organize this mutual aid system, but once that has been settled, the rest of the task is a matter of making sure that each person pulls her weight. There is considerable joy taken in this process; working together as a team creates a strong sense of belonging, and of being a little stronger as a member of a group rather than as a solitary individual.

Parental support

The fact that children have an inborn urge to cooperate does not mean that they are immune to parental example. If a small child witnesses acts of great kindness on the part of her mother or father, she will be influenced by these acts and will want to emulate them. Conversely, if she witnesses acts of cruelty and selfishness on the part of her parents or her older siblings, she may start to doubt her own naturally developing feelings of kindness and a conflict will grow in her that she will, later on, find hard to resolve.

The little mother

One of the most unselfish forms of human behaviour is the way in which a mother gives herself up to the rearing of her new baby. Maternal care is perhaps the least selfish of all human instincts and it is surprising how this same urge can begin to reveal itself even in a very young girl. A tiny girl can be found gently and carefully feeding her doll and talking to it in a soft voice. A little later, when she has a new baby brother or sister, she will show the same care towards the new addition to the family. True, this is partly in imitation of what she sees her mother doing, but it is more than that. A small boy may witness the same maternal love, but is not moved to emulate it. It seems as if the human female is so strongly programmed to care for babies, that the drive to do so starts to show itself, even in a 5-year-old.

In some countries where poverty is rife, 'little mothers' can be seen taking charge of babies while their parents are away trying to earn a living. The serious intent written on the face of a 'little mother' as she stands with a baby slung on her hip, waiting for her real mother or father to come home with a little food, is a heartbreaking testimony to the kindness and loving care of which the human being is capable.

first friends

If a 2-year-old has a friend it is probably because she was placed next to the other child at a party or in a playgroup. Generally, 2-year-olds do not actively seek out friends. That comes later. The earliest age is 2½, but for most children it does not happen until they are 3.

Making friends

One of the problems facing the friend-maker is that, being ignorant of the subtleties of such relationships, she either acts too strongly or too weakly. She either overwhelms the other child with too much attention, or underwhelms him with too little. Getting the right balance is something that has to be learnt gradually, through trial and error.

Parental help with this problem does not usually work too well. If one child is naturally high-spirited and the other is rather quiet, the two will find it difficult to strike up a balanced relationship. If a parent tries to encourage one child to be quieter or more energetic to facilitate a balance, this is asking the very young child to modify her natural personality in a way that is unlikely to last. It is better for each child to seek out another that has about the same level of energy and shared interests.

This need for balance was confirmed by a study of slightly older children between the ages of 3 and 5. It was found that the majority had a special friend. When the behaviour of mutual friends was examined, it emerged that each pair had similar levels of assertiveness and 'peer competence' – the ability to handle a friendship well. In other words, even from a very early age, like seeks out like.

Making mistakes

There is a lot to learn about making friendships that last. Parents have to help out by introducing certain courtesies that they themselves take for granted, such as saying hello and goodbye, please and thank you. And they must be wary of too much aggression entering a relationship. Pushing and shoving and hitting may seem like fun or an acceptable way of resolving a difference, but friendships can quickly flounder if such actions become commonplace.

It is important to recognize two distinct types of aggression between young friends, especially between boys. If one boy, with a serious, frowning face, hits another one, the blow may be minor, but it is serious and is read as such by the victim. On the other hand, violent rough-and-tumble actions may occur that appear much worse to the outsider, but if the two participants are laughing or smiling as they fight, then each recognizes that the aggression is not real but only playful. Even at a very early age, the child uses the smile as a defusing signal in this way.

There are three common kinds of aggression that cause serious rifts in friendships between the very young. These are the snatch, the direct insult, and the indirect insult. The snatch is the grabbing or forcible taking of a toy being used by the companion. The direct insult usually takes the form of criticizing the way the friend is tackling a task and implying that the speaker could do it better. The indirect insult is the hostile gossip, in which harsh things are said about a friend behind her back. A small child may not feel she is doing anything too terrible with these actions or words, and often fails to understand why her companion is reacting so strongly to them. The pre-school child's urge to make friends precedes any delicacy in handling those friendships. In this, she needs all the help she can get from her parents, who, as gently as possible, must educate her in the niceties of conduct that is more appealing and attractive to others.

sharing and taking turns

Parents want their children to be kind and generous and to understand the concepts of sharing and taking turns, so they are often dismayed at the absence of these ideas from the world of the typical 2-year-old. Patience is needed, because it takes at least two more years before the child fully appreciates the views and feelings of his companions. Only then will he be prepared to initiate sharing and be willing to take turns as a matter of course.

Personal toys

Parents who try to rush the pre-school child into a generous frame of mind will probably have the opposite effect. If a child is forced to share his precious, favourite toys with other children he may, in desperation, become more selfish rather than less so. He feels his personal belongings are not his, after all, and must therefore defend his ownership against what he now perceives as a hostile adult world. His parents own a house, a car, furniture and all the rest, whereas he only owns a few special toys. They are his only property and he enjoys his possession of them as a sign that he is, at least, in control of a few things in his environment. If a visiting child is given his toys to play with and breaks one of them, he suddenly feels his 'private territory' threatened and reacts badly. In a similar way, if a thoughtless parent throws away on old toy of his without consulting him, he again feels that his tiny 'power base' has been unfairly attacked.

The solution to this problem is for each child to have his own personal toys, available only to him, with a special box or place in which they are always kept when not in use. Only he has control over these objects. In addition, there must be other, communal, toys that he accepts are not his personal property, but are also to be made available to siblings or visiting children. With these two categories of toy the child comes to understand that some things in life are private and others are to be shared. Because his exclusive ownership of the private toys is fully recognized, he is then more willing to share the others.

Play-school sharing

Some playgroups follow a similar pattern. If a child brings a favourite toy from home (often to give him a sense of security by having a familiar object with him), his carers provide him with a special place to keep it and make it clear that it is not for general sharing. Toys and other apparatus supplied by the playgroup are, however, for communal use and for sharing. If there is a dispute about who gets to ride in the pedal car or sit on the swing, then a waiting list is made and the first child on the list is told that he may play with the toy for as long as he likes. When he has finished, the next name on the list is called out and she now takes her turn, and so on down the list. This becomes the child's first experience of the principle of sharing and taking turns. It starts a trend that eventually leads to one child spontaneously offering to share a toy with another. Once this major step has been taken, it is only a matter of time before the other child reciprocates, offering another toy in exchange. Now the concept of swapping or trading has appeared on the scene and gradually, little by little, the world of the pre-schooler becomes one in which mutual aid and kindness start to play a significant role.

Those parents who have followed the regime of recognizing the right of a pre-school child to own personal property, over which he has sole control, have reported that later in life their child has shared more generously than the offspring of parents who ignored this principle.

towards cooperation

Compared to toddlers experiencing the terrible twos (see pages 120–121), by the age of 3, a child shows a marked change in her social behaviour. The frequency of aggressive acts begins to drop. She becomes friendlier towards her companions, with more cooperative actions. With the majority of individuals, this trend continues for the rest of their lives. It has been estimated that this is true of about 95 per cent of the population. The other 5 per cent retain the antisocial urges of the 2-year-old, becoming a potential danger to society.

How important is teaching?

There are two views as to why humans become increasingly friendly as they grow older. According to the environmental school, this change is due solely to early teaching. They believe that human beings are born violent and that babies would be even more violent than 2-year-old toddlers if only they had the muscular equipment to carry out aggressive acts. The peak in violence at the age of 2, they claim, is the result of the fact that, for the first time in her life, the tiny toddler now has the muscular ability to kick, bite, slap, push and hit. The reduction in this violence as she grows older is thought to be entirely owing to careful teaching on the part of adults, who demonstrate to her the advantages of sharing and cooperation.

Others refuse to accept that teaching is the only reason why we become increasingly friendly and nonviolent as we progress from 2 to 5 years old. This view sees the decline in

violence as a genetically programmed trend in which the young child becomes increasingly susceptible to being taught the rules of society. This increased susceptibility is not the result of teaching but is thought to be an essential part of human nature.

It is argued that the human species, in order to survive in primeval times, had to increase cooperative behaviour following the switch to hunting as a way of life. To succeed on the hunt, the males of the human tribe had to cooperate actively with one another. And, because of the division of labour between the sexes, males and females also had to cooperate to a greater degree. This meant that the more ancient aggressive tendencies had to be tamed during the course of evolution, if we were to succeed as a species. This taming would become increasingly necessary as growing children reached a stage where they had the muscle power that could do serious harm. The 2-year-old human is too weak to do much harm, reducing the need for the taming process until after that age is passed.

The role of the nursery school

There is a lot to be said for the nursery-school environment in which a child is encouraged to absorb the social skills of interacting with other children, and not to focus too heavily on rapid academic progress. While the child in such a situation may not hone her academic skills, she will almost certainly improve her emotional life and become far more sociable, ready for schooldays.

There is some evidence to support the idea that a nursery school that allows the child to have more fun and games equips her better for the future than the more academic playgroups. It is said that a child from a more playful group can easily catch up academically with others when both types reach the next stage in education, whereas a child from a more academic group never manages to catch up socially or emotionally. In other words, the pre-school phase of growing up is earmarked by evolution for maturing social skills and these should be given priority, with academic skills coming later in formal schooling.

socio-dramatic play

One of the most complicated forms of childhood play is that of creating a game that involves the acting out of dramatic scenes or social events with others. Called socio-dramatic play, this requires the child to adopt a fictional role and then to act accordingly. While pretending to be someone else, the child must stick to the script that he has devised for himself. He cannot suddenly decide to break from character and be himself, because that would spoil the illusion created by the game. This means that socio-dramatic play is an important way for a child to learn self-control without having it imposed upon him by adults.

Sources of dramatic play

A child borrows his dramas from what he observes in the adult world around him. For example, a 5-year-old decides to invent a medical drama in which he is the doctor and his toy animals, friends or siblings are his patients. He may have visited a relative in hospital, watched a medical drama on television or observed the serious mood that descended on the house when a little brother was ill and visited at home by the family doctor. Using this as a basis for his own story line, he sets about creating a hospital ward or a sick room and, using his own imagination, re-creates the drama of curing the sick and tending the wounded, talking to them in his best bedside manner and using props to assist his rounds.

One of the strangest cases of socio-dramatic play involved two real sisters who would play-act at being two imaginary, ideal sisters. In real life they sometimes argued, sometimes ignored one another and sometimes were very friendly. In other words, their natural behaviour was as varied and spontaneous as that of any other pair of sisters. However, when they were playing at being ideal sisters, their behaviour was much more strictly controlled. Now they behaved as much like one another as possible, even wearing the same clothes and talking in the same kind of voice. During the play-acting they always loved one another and saw themselves as a very special pair, quite superior to everyone else. As real sisters, they took life as it came, but as ideal sisters they imposed upon themselves a tight set of rules of conduct and, with considerable mental effort, forced themselves to follow their self-imposed conditions as closely as possible.

Self-imposed rules

The more play of this kind that a child invents, the more he comes to understand self-restraint and self-discipline – qualities that he will find so useful as he grows older and has to attend social gatherings, where he must control himself and inhibit his sudden impulses and natural urges. At school, teachers are sometimes surprised by the extent to which a very young child follows the rules on stage when taking part in a school play; early socio-dramatic play has something to do with this.

Part of the appeal of early play-dramas is that the rules are made by the player himself and can therefore be designed to feed his own private fantasies. And part of their appeal is that, unlike formal games, these invented dramas can be started and stopped at will, whenever the player feels like it. There is a 'time in' when the game is on, and a 'time out' when the play must stop for some emergency (like visiting the bathroom or taking a snack), an adult interruption or simply because the child has for the moment grown tired of the game.

This ability to self-regulate the length of the game, to start and stop and start again at will, is the key difference between the informal play-dramas of early childhood and the formal games of later childhood. Once the small child joins a team playing football or some other such sport, he must then be prepared to accept the referee's whistle, rather than his own change of mood, as the play-breaker. But if he has experienced a rich pre-school life of his own brand of socio-dramatic play, he will find the adult versions much easier to accept and to enjoy.

playing by the rules

During the course of play, children start to introduce rules that lead them, eventually, to enjoy structured games with a fixed pattern. At first, the rules are so simple that they are easy to remember. With musical chairs, for example, there are only two rules: keep moving round the chairs while the music is playing and sit down when it stops. The removal of one chair with each round is not a rule, but something that the adults do. And before the age of 6, playing by the rules rarely gets beyond games of this level of simplicity.

Breaking the rules

The pre-school child enjoys obeying a very simple rule, such as all falling down together at the right moment in a nursery rhyme. More complex rules are not common or popular before the start of formal schooling. A game with rigid, adult-imposed rules may start out well enough, but the bubbling playfulness of the pre-school child may soon rebel and she will then introduce some new variation of her own invention into a game that is not supposed to have impromptu modifications. One parent tells the story of how she taught a very young child to play draughts. All went well until, bored by the monotony of the actions and the rigidity of the rules, the small boy picked up one of the pieces and, holding it aloft, shouted 'super-draught', whereupon he dashed it down across the board, sending all the other pieces flying. His idea of combining the concept of a superhero with a game like draughts reveals how the spontaneously inventive brain of the pre-schooler resents being tamed into repetitive orderliness.

The rules of the game

This clash between playing by the rules and breaking the rules is the essence of adult inventiveness. The man who invented the razor blade was able to shout 'super-blade' and sweep away all the old cut-throat razors. Then the man who invented the electric razor was able to shout 'super-blade' again and sweep away the razor blades. In the play of the pre-school child one can see this progression at work, as each new play pattern is replaced by something new. The brain repeatedly enjoys, first the discovery of a new rule, then the refinement of behaviour within the limits of that rule, and then, finally, the breaking of that rule and the introduction of a new one.

What we see in the play development of small children often repeats what has happened in adult life. For example, the tiny child loves playing with a ball because it offers her a magnified reward. That is to say, it only takes a small action to make it move a long distance. The first encounter with a ball is puzzling, because it moves in unexpected ways. The child throws and hits it more or less randomly, then gradually learns how to control its movements. Soon the child subjects the hitting or throwing or catching to some kind of organization to invent simple ball games. Then she adds targets – goals or baskets into which she must throw, kick or place the ball. Little by little she introduces a ball game involving a number of players, although the rules are still rather vague. Then the rules become tighter. Eventually a referee or an umpire is added to ensure that the rules are always obeyed, and we arrive at the formal game. This is like a repeat of the history of football, where the rough-and-tumble street game of past centuries became the formal school game on a proper pitch. Out of that game grew all the adult games we now have, such as soccer, rugby, American football, Australian rules, Gaelic football and the rest. All of these began, originally, as a simple play pattern enjoyed by 2-year-old children when they first discovered that a spherical object has a huge potential for varied movement when it is struck.

boredom

Two kinds of stress can cause problems for the pre-school child. The first is over-stimulation, in which the world of the child is suddenly overloaded in some way. This may be caused by a violent incident of some kind – a family tragedy – or simply an overdose of novel stimulation to the point at which the child feels he can no longer cope. The second kind of stress is the exact opposite, and is caused by severe under-stimulation. And the boredom of under-stimulation can be just as damaging to a young child as the chaos of over-stimulation.

A need for novelty

From the age of 2 to the age of 5, there is a growing need for novelty in everyday life. The small child's curiosity, and his urge to explore his exciting new world, become stronger with each passing day. As his body grows and his brain matures, he becomes increasingly eager to investigate everything and anything that comes his way. True, he needs to do this from a safe base, from a familiar setting, but within that secure framework there is a powerful need to try out something he has not done before. It is this inborn inquisitiveness that has been the making of our species and has led us from living in tiny tribes in mud huts to forming the huge civilizations that populate the great cities. And it starts very early, just as soon as a child has the muscle power to put it into practice. But what happens if the child is not given the chance to express this very basic urge?

The sterile environment

For most parents, helping a child to satisfy his curiosity is one of the great joys of raising a family. It does, however, cost the parents a great deal of time and energy, and some adults cannot cope with this. If, for whatever reason, they themselves are in a state of crisis or misery, they may have little energy to spare. They may see to the basic survival needs of their offspring – feeding him, keeping him warm and seeing that he gets a good night's sleep – but when it comes to creative playtime they simply cannot be bothered. They may provide a few toys, but these soon lose their appeal, and the child is left to amuse himself in an unchanging, unstimulating, sterile environment. In such cases, boredom soon sets in. If this condition becomes prolonged it can seriously retard both the child's intellectual development and his emotional growth.

The reaction to boredom

Children react to prolonged periods of boredom in several ways. Some give up the struggle, become withdrawn and mope. They may try inventing fantasies and daydreams to occupy their minds, but they eventually tire of this strategy. Others become hostile and destructive, attempting to introduce novelty into a boring environment by inflicting physical damage on it. Still others do their best to attract attention, becoming loud and noisy and deliberately difficult, simply to break the monotony. For them it may be the only way they can gain parental attention. The attention may be scolding, but even that is better than no attention at all. All these responses prove conclusively that the pre-schooler's brain abhors a vacuum and will do anything to avoid periods of acute boredom.

Avoiding boredom

It is simple enough to relieve boredom. All that is necessary is to provide a rich environment full of exciting toys and games and someone with whom these playthings can be enjoyed. This is easy to say, but for a busy parent there is sometimes no time or energy to spare and the child's need for lively interaction goes unanswered. If this is only an occasional problem, the child is resilient enough to recover from these setbacks and makes up for lost time later on. Prolonged and intense boredom for a pre-school child may, however, cause long-term damage.

family relationships

There are several very different family scenarios: the large, extended family; the nuclear family; the single parent family; the blended family with its combination of step-children and possibly half-brothers and sisters, to name but a few, that a pre-school child may face. The luckiest child is clearly one with a loving mother and father who also love one another. A variant is the home in which both parents love the child but are at war with one another. An extension of this sees the parents separate, leaving the pre-school child living as a one-parent family. A slightly different version of this is when one parent dies.

A new scenario sees a child reared by a single woman who, following conception, chooses to be alone. Another recent situation has the child reared by two women or by two men living as couples. And finally there is the tragedy of the child who loses both parents and must be reared in an orphanage, or with adoptive parents. How do these different scenarios affect the development of the child?

Role models

To every pre-school child, the adults who feed her, protect her, play with her and educate her are of crucial importance. She may have a set of inborn aids that help her to develop as a successful young human being, but without adult support and guidance she will not survive. Studies of young children growing up in small tribal societies reveal that they benefit from very close attention from their mothers, from play sessions with their fathers, from constant mixing with the other small children, and from elderly aunts and grandmothers who are always present to provide back-up. Strangers are almost entirely absent.

That ancient way of life is very different from the modern urban situation in which each family lives cut off from others, in separate houses or apartments in towns and cities that are crowded with thousands of strangers. Inside each of these modern homes, a child must grow and develop without many of the social benefits of the ancient tribal existence. Extended families have declined dramatically, with aunts, uncles and grandparents often living far away. In addition, single-parent families have become much more common. What does all this mean for the developing child?

The primary carer

Careful studies have revealed that the most important factor in the life of a pre-school child is having one loving, primary carer. It seems that human children are programmed to develop a powerful attachment to just one adult – the mother figure. In almost all cases, the mother figure is also the biological mother, but in rare cases where the mother is dead or not available for some unusual reason, another figure can take her place. What apparently causes confusion is if there are several mother figures, none of whom takes the clear role of the dominant carer. The child's brain seems to have a priority mechanism, requiring one adult to be the key figure and others to play supporting roles.

In a traditional family, the father is the second most-important figure. Occasionally, a modern family may consist of a successful working mother and a stay-at-home father. In such instances, the ultimate test is to see which adult a child runs to for a comforting hug when upset.

The quality of caring

Given all the different family permutations, which is the best arrangement for the developing pre-school child? The answer is simple. Given the two following conditions, any arrangements can work well enough: for the first 5 years of life, a child must have one primary carer; and the child must be able to enjoy plenty of quality time with his carer. Quality time is not just loving time – although that is essential – but is time spent interacting, playing together, learning things together, exploring things together and talking together. Providing a child has that kind of family relationship, all should be well.

siblings and rivalry

Family photographs rarely tell the whole truth. The group of happy faces, mother, father and their small children, all smiling together for the camera, only tells a partial truth. Yes, they can all be cheerful together, but there are many other times when brothers and sisters are at war with one another. Sibling rivalry is a very real factor of family life and, even with the best parenting, cannot be avoided altogether. Fortunately the rows and disputes are usually short-lived and peace soon returns to the home – for a while at least.

Sibling rivalry is part of the natural dynamics of a family, with each child competing for attention and to establish themselves as individuals. Birth order affects relationships (see pages 22–23) between children, and their parents, and a child can feel jealous of the arrival of a new sibling as early as 18-months. Age differences between children will influence their responses and behaviour, and rivalry can continue throughout childhood.

What causes the rivalry?

There are two kinds of dispute between siblings. The first is caused when, say, a 2-year-old does not understand the need to share something with a 4-year-old. The latter, having just discovered the rules of sharing and taking turns is outraged to find that they do not seem to apply to his little 2-year-old brother. If he wants a toy he takes it and that is that. He cannot grasp the need to allow the older child also to play with it.

The second kind of dispute concerns rivalry for the attention of a parent. If two small children both want to play with their mother or father, a careful balancing act has to be performed by the parent, ensuring that each child feels he or she has enjoyed an equal amount of loving care. This is not an easy trick for parents to pull off, especially if they have a large family of small children. If three children have all been busy painting pictures, they often show the finished works to a parent and demand to know which one is the best. This is a minefield for the unwary parent. If he or she tells the truth, namely that one picture is much better then the other two, one child will be happy and two will feel unloved. If the parent says they are all very good, the children know they are being short-changed and each

one will think it is because his particular picture was so awful that the parent had to lie to please everyone. Children, even very small children, are fully aware of diplomatic parental deceit. Parents eventually learn special tricks, like suggesting that all three pictures must be put on a wall together and then visitors can vote for the one they like best. Delaying tactics of this kind usually mean that the whole contest is forgotten.

A third kind of sibling rivalry is a rather unpleasant kind and not always easy to detect or to handle. In a large family one small child may take a long-term dislike to another. He may then begin a secret campaign of upsetting the other, usually smaller one. When no parents are around, he will maliciously interfere with a game the smaller sibling has just settled down to enjoy. When the little one starts screaming the culprit is nowhere to be seen. It is not hard for a parent to uncover this type of rivalry and deal with it, but it does take up valuable time and effort and has to be handled with sensitivity.

In the long run, many of these sibling problems resolve themselves and genuine bonds of attachment develop between a particular brother and sister or, more likely, between a sister and a sister. Bonds between brother and brother are less common.

Problems from outside the family can help to create a 'blood is thicker than water' mentality, in which one sibling defends another one from external interference. There is an old Arabic saying: 'I am against my brother; my brother and I are against my cousin; I, my brother, and my cousin are against the stranger.'

humour and laughter

All humour is based on the giving or receiving of a safe shock. To be funny, someone must break a rule, but in such a way that we feel completely safe. If a parent hides behind a cushion, then lowers the cushion and goes 'boo', an infant will gurgle with laughter. If a stranger does the same thing, the infant may cry out in fear. In both cases, the sudden 'boo' frightens the child, but when she sees a totally trusted parent, she knows that the shock is safe and performs that strangely segmented version of a cry that we call laughter.

The function of humour

If a small child plays a hiding game in which she leaps out on a playful parent who pretends to be terrified, the child laughs uproariously at the adult's panic. Then, if role reversal occurs and the parent hides and leaps out on the child, the child pretends to be frightened in the same way. Again, there is laughter. These safe shocks may be repeated many times before the child tires of the game. When she does so, she will feel happy and relaxed, because prolonged laughter releases feel-good chemicals into the blood.

Tests have shown that, the more humour there is in a child's life, the fewer disturbed moods she has. She is generally less anxious and experiences less tension in ordinary day-to-day activities. In addition, her relationship with those close to her is more friendly and her social interactions with others less aggressive. This is why humour has been referred to as a 'social lubricant'.

Types of humour

There are three types of humour:
Responsive humour: when someone makes a child laugh.
Productive humour: when the child initiates the fun herself and makes someone else laugh.
Aggressive humour: when the child laughs at someone else, or when someone else laughs at the child. Bullying in a playgroup may involve being laughed at, although this unpleasant type of humour is more likely to occur later in the school playground than in the early playgroup.

Among pre-school children, humour appears most often in vigorous games involving such things as chasing, hiding, catching and wrestling; in moments of triumph when the child laughs with joy at having conquered a difficult task or won a competition; and when something incongruous and unexpected happens. A playful adult who suddenly appears wearing a funny mask or a silly hat, may make the child laugh simply because the action breaks one of the social rules that the child has just started to learn.

Another kind of humour occurs when something unlikely occurs, and the more improbable it is, the funnier it is. If a child is playing alone, for example, building a tower of bricks, and the tower falls over so that one of the bricks lands on the head of the family dog who is asleep, the sheer improbability of the action makes the child laugh out loud, even though she is alone. If, on the other hand, she has some of her friends with her, she laughs louder, and if they all join in, her laughter increases even more. There is a powerful social factor in humour, making it an infectious activity that helps to synchronize the mood of a small group and make them feel closer to one another than they did before the incident. For this reason, social laughter in playgroups is an important force in improving relationships.

Jokes

Verbal jokes become popular with 3-year-olds, as their language skills begin to develop. They find it funny to say 'hello mummy' to daddy or 'hello kitty' to the family dog. Visual humour is also common, with a child adding a tail and whiskers to a drawing of a man. For the pre-school child, however, there are several kinds of humour that are still beyond her, such as sarcasm or irony and the telling of jokes. When she does try to tell a joke, copying an older child, she usually gets the ending wrong. These forms of humour must await the school years.

trauma and anxiety

Specialists who study childhood traumas recognize five kinds of anxiety disorder. They are referred to as 'generalized anxiety disorder', 'obsessive compulsive disorder', 'panic disorder', 'post-traumatic stress disorder' and 'separation anxiety disorder'.

Generalized anxiety disorder

Even at a very young age, a child may become a chronic worrier or fretter. Instead of being excited by the possibility of exploring new activities and enjoying new experiences, he senses hidden risks and dangers in all of them. There are no specific phobias, but rather a general feeling that everything that is about to happen is potentially harmful.

This state of mind can seriously inhibit a child's curiosity and his natural urge to investigate the world around him. In some cases this condition can be traced to the unintentional impact of an unusually anxious parent. If a child senses prolonged, intense agitation in, say, an otherwise caring mother, his brain tells him that, since he has complete trust in his loving parent, her fears must be justified. He develops a sympathetic anxiety, even though he himself has nothing to worry about.

Unfortunately, children are so sensitive to the emotional moods of their parents that it is extremely difficult for adults to hide their feelings, no matter how hard they try. This is true even at the baby stage, where the classic example is of the agitated mother who cannot stop her baby crying, but then hands the child to a placid grandmother who restores calm in a matter of moments.

Obsessive compulsive disorder

An obsession is something that a child does not wish to focus on, but which refuses to go away. Despite himself, he cannot get it out of his mind. A compulsion is the action that his obsession makes him perform. A child suffering from an obsessive compulsive disorder finds that his concentration is repeatedly interrupted, as his mind keeps dragging him back to his unwanted preoccupation. His sleep may also be disrupted, as he wakes up in the night to dwell once more on his uninvited obsession.

Panic disorder

Panic attacks involve a sudden loss of normal control in a social situation. Even the most basic bodily functions cease to operate in the usual way. Breathing becomes laboured, the heart beats faster, there is excessive sweating, temperature control goes from one extreme to the other, with flushing and shivering, the body may shake or tremble and there may be a feeling of dizziness. These panic attacks usually occur in what is perceived to be a threatening social situation, something that the child unconsciously feels he cannot face. Once attacks of this kind have occurred, there is then the added fear that another will occur and this compounds the problem, with the result that the child may become increasingly antisocial as he tries to avoid them.

Post-traumatic stress disorder

Children between the ages of 2 and 5 who experience a terrifying ordeal or a major family tragedy find it hard to accept what has happened. 'When is mummy coming back?' is one of the hardest questions to answer. Some children become emotionally numb, others fretful and fearful, and nightmares are common. Eventually, the child recovers and gets on with his life, but in some cases the memory of the trauma lies buried deep inside the brain and may resurface in some damaging form many years later.

Separation anxiety disorder

In some cases a child panics when he is separated from his primary carer. He has a deep-seated fear that something terrible will happen to him if he is taken away and he does everything he can to resist. This anxiety is an exaggeration of the normal attachment a child feels towards the adult who has looked after him. If he is forced to endure separation, he may suffer from a variety of ailments, such as headaches, sleeplessness and stomach upsets.

fears and phobias

At the age of 4, a child may sometimes develop irrational fears and phobias that are hard for the adult to understand. It is as if she has a built-in warning system that works in opposition to her intense curiosity. The curiosity drives her on to investigate almost everything she encounters and enables her to make new discoveries every day. The phobias ensure that a few of the novel elements in her environment are, instead, avoided at all costs.

The arrival of phobias

The reason that phobias do not develop before the age of 4 is because they have evolved as powerful protection devices that shield a child from risk at the stage when she starts to become seriously mobile. In a primitive tribal world, the 4-year-old is liable to wander off on her own and meet very real dangers, such as poisonous spiders and venomous snakes. If her playful curiosity drove her on to investigate these strange animals she might easily die as a result. This fear is so deeply embedded that, from a tender age, children fear both spiders and snakes.

There are two theories as to how this comes about. One sees snake and spider phobias as inborn; the other sees it as a universal teaching by adults who make horrified sounds when they see a film or picture of a snake or a large spider. What is unusual about this teaching – if that is how children do develop these particular phobias – is that they react to it much more strongly than they do to other things. For example, if a child knocks over a bottle of ink, the parent may make exactly the same kind of horrified noises, but the child is hardly likely to develop a fear of ink in later life. It is as if the brain of the child is primed ready to have a fear of snakes or spiders implanted, leading to serious phobias for many individuals later in life.

Traumas causing phobias

It is rare for a child to get through her first 5 years without experiencing at least a few traumatic moments. The intrepid explorer who climbs up high and is then too frightened to climb down again and has to be rescued with a great deal of fuss, may well develop a fear of heights. The child who falls into a river and is nearly drowned, but is then rescued with a great deal of fuss, may well develop a fear of water. The child who talks to a stranger and is then dragged away by a panic-stricken parent, may later develop an acute, overwhelming fear of strangers.

In the first two of these three examples there are two crucial elements present – a frightening event and the great fuss that is made about it. Both elements are important in creating the later phobia. If the adult had made light of the drama instead of dramatizing it, it might not have led to a later, powerful fear. The third example is significant in this respect. Initially the child was not frightened, and if the parent had simply told her not to talk to strangers in future, there might have been a simple learning process, with the child becoming slightly more cautious. But if the adult goes into a state of blind panic, the child registers this reaction and her brain files it away for future reference.

The common phobias

One study of 4-year-olds revealed that no fewer than two out of three had some kind of powerful, recurrent fear. Among the most common fears were: snakes, spiders, heights, large animals, loud noises, strangers, darkness, ghosts, monsters, confined spaces, public spaces and certain foods. Parents of 4- and 5-year-olds are often exasperated when they find that their children suddenly refuse point blank to eat a particular kind of food. The food itself may have been consumed happily the day before. Then, overnight, it is taboo. If they could see inside the child's mind, they would be puzzled to find that she has decided that this food is poisonous. In a primeval situation there were plenty of poisonous fungi and berries that had to be avoided. It would seem that these strange modern reactions to harmless foodstuffs are a misfiring of an ancient survival mechanism.

a sense of justice

One of the most powerful emotions experienced by the young child is the feeling that he has been treated unjustly. The cry of 'that's not fair!' is one of the most heartfelt complaints to be heard in the family home. From a very early age a child develops a powerful sense of justice and fair play and when he is the victim of some kind of inconsistency or a breaking of the rules that he has come to accept, he is liable to collapse in floods of tears.

Broken promises

One of the worst punishments a small child can receive is a broken promise when the change of plan is beyond his control and has not been caused by anything he has done. The father who promises to take his little son to a football match and then forgets about it or makes other plans, or the mother who promises to take her small daughter to a fancy dress party and then finds she is too busy to do so, hurt their offspring perhaps more than they realize. Astonishingly, although adults find that they have forgotten most of the day-to-day details of their first 5 years of life, it is moments of deep, hurtful disappointment like these that linger on in the memory.

Being cheated

Another kind of persistent memory is of the moment when a child is cheated, either by an adult or by another child. At nursery school, when a toy is broken and the culprit accuses an innocent friend of causing the damage, that false accusation may cause acute distress of a kind that is hard for the victim to express. Matters are made worse if the adult in charge believes the lie and the innocent victim is then punished for something he did not do. This will probably be a moment of injustice that he will never forget and may return to haunt him and even influence his adult behaviour in later life. The fact that the culprit made the false accusation because he was scared of owning up, possibly owing to the harsh way he had been punished for such misdeeds at home, never enters the head of the victim and would probably provide little comfort even if it did.

Parental cheating can also cause anger, as when a younger brother or sister is unfairly favoured in some competition. The older child has done especially well and deserves praise, but because the siblings are younger and need help, they are the ones who receive the special treatment from the well-meaning parent. The older child then feels there is no point in trying hard because he cannot win. Or each child is told that he will get a chance to have a turn at something they all enjoy, but in the end there isn't time and one of them gets left out. These moments can cause acute disappointment, not just because one child misses the fun, but because he misses the fun that all the others are allowed to enjoy. The excuse that time has run out fails to mollify him and he feels that he has been unjustly treated. Maintaining consistent rewards among a lively group of siblings is a difficult balancing act for any parent.

Betrayal by a friend

Another moment of acute distress for a 4- or 5-year-old occurs when a little friend draws attention to something wrong that he has done. If he has had a small accident and is trying to hide it, and his neighbour shouts out 'Miss, Miss, look what Charlie has done!' and then he is punished for it, the feeling of resentment at having been so publicly betrayed can be intense.

The roots of justice

These three insults – the broken promise, being cheated and the betrayal – cause outrage in a child because, by the age of 5, he has already developed a sense of justice and understands the concept of playing by the rules. Once parents lay down a set of behaviour rules, a child expects them to be followed as closely as possible, as the parents expect the child to respect and abide by them. Above all, he expects consistency and fair play, and the innate sense of cooperation that has been locked into the parental rule system rebels whenever inconsistencies occur.

conclusion

Watching a self-absorbed, stubborn, clumsy 2-year-old son or daughter grow into a wonderfully cooperative, talkative, athletic and cheerful 5-year-old is one of the greatest joys of parenthood. These early years are a time of great discovery, of boundless curiosity and endless play. The joyful freedom of expression that is experienced in these pre-school days will never be repeated.

The taming of the toddler

When the helpless baby gets to his feet and becomes mobile, the world is there to be conquered and he sets about this task as forcefully as he can, often becoming frustrated by his own inadequacies. Stubbornly he forges ahead, trying to make his mark and learn everything he can about the exciting new environment in which he finds himself. As the months pass, he becomes more and more communicative, thanks to the astonishing human ability to convert sounds into words and then assemble words into sentences. At the same time, his limbs become stronger and his manual control more refined. Every day offers new challenges and he has a powerful exploratory urge to drive him on and on. If he is not punished for his energetic activities and if his environment is rich, he will spend the next few years programming his brain in a way that will last him a lifetime.

Leaving the nest

If he has been lucky during his progression from 2 years to 5 he will end up as an optimistic, intelligent, self-assured, articulate being when the first day of school arrives and he sets forth on his long period of formal education. It will not all be plain sailing, however, because he must now be prepared to subject himself to more rigid rules and repetitive routines than he has been used to. Adult society will require him to suppress to some extent the imaginative playfulness that has so dominated his earliest years, and formal schooling will begin pushing him in this direction. He will have to learn that play, instead of being everywhere, is now going to be restricted to a strange new place called a playground, or to something else called 'free time'. He will now have to accept an unfamiliar and unpleasant distinction between work and play. Before, all work was

play and all play was work, but now he will find them being squeezed into two different compartments. If he is fortunate, he will find that his teachers encourage a certain amount of creative playfulness during the hours of schoolwork, but he will also discover that playtime is no longer quite as free and easy as it once was. There may be times when he will suffer from boredom and feel disenchanted with the new phase of life he has entered, but modern society is so complex and so demanding that only a prolonged period of carefully structured formal education will fit him out for it when he eventually becomes an adult.

Fortunately, his young skull contains the best brain in the animal kingdom and two of its more remarkable qualities are its adaptability and its resilience. Even if he finds some of his youthful enthusiasm crushed by the weight of cultural indoctrination, he will find ways of fighting back. And one thing is certain, the greater the richness of experience he has enjoyed in his pre-school years, the greater his chances of maintaining a sense of wonder and imaginative creativity in the years ahead. He may not remember all the magical details of those first 5 years of life, but they will have left their mark and will have made him whatever it is that, as a young adult, he turns out to be.

index

acknowledgements

Author's acknowledgements:

I would like to express my enormous debt to my wife Ramona for her tireless research that kept me up to date with all the latest reports on this fascinating subject. And a special thanks to my grandchildren for once again bringing me face to face with the reality of what it is to be experiencing the first years of life on this exciting planet.

My thanks also to Jane McIntosh and Charlotte Macey of Hamlyn, whose contribution to this book far exceeds what one might expect from its editors. The whole concept and structure of the book is theirs, and I am extremely grateful to them for their tremendous enthusiasm for the whole project.

I would also like to acknowledge the splendid contribution of Penny Stock and Janis Utton whose wonderful visual designs have made this volume such a feast for the eyes. And finally, my thanks to my literary agent, Silke Bruenink, for her expert help in setting up this project.

Executive Editor Jane McIntosh
Senior Editor Charlotte Macey
Executive Art Director Penny Stock
Designer Janis Utton
Production Manager David Hearn
Picture Researcher Emma O'Neil

Contributor to concertina section: Suzanne Milne.

Picture credits

Alamy/Blue Jean Images 151 bottom right; /fotoshoot 39 bottom left; /Carson Ganci 27; /Jean Lannen 92; /Picture Partners 74-75; /VStock 57. **Corbis**/Eric Audras/PhotoAlto 101 right; /Heide Benser 21, 35 bottom right, 81 top right, 140 top, 140 bottom; /Bloomimage 39 top left, 42, 55, 66-67, 91 bottom left, 100 left, 117, 154 top left; /Sandro di Carlo Darsa/PhotoAlto 8-9; /Dex Images, Inc. 101 left, 103; /Nick Dolding 81 top left; /Floresco Productions 81 bottom right; /Monalyn Gracia 129; /A. Inden 65 top; /Roy McMahon 15 top left; /Roberto Melchiorre 81 bottom left; /Bruno Obmann 96 top; /Studio DL 71; /Miao Wang 130; **Getty Images**/Absodels 77 bottom right; /Janie Airey 19 bottom right; /Natalie Avakian 153; /Peter Beavis 19 top right; /BLOOMimage 28, 35 top left, 69, 77 bottom left, 114; /Milena Boniek 24; /Lauren Burke 16 bottom right; /Nancy Brown 123; /Compassionate Eye Foundation/Inti St. Clair 93; /Mieke Dalle 39 top right, 82-83; /Doable/A.collection 104; /George Doyle 96 bottom right; /Julia Fishkin 7 top right; /Lena Granefelt 136; /Mimi Haddon 7 bottom left, 77 top left; /Tim Hale 41; /Mark Hall 127; /Meredith Heuer 158; /Michael Hitoshi 157; /David Hofmann 65 bottom; /Nancy Honey 163; /Indeed 109; /JGI 100 right; /JGI/Jamie Grill 25; /Chad Johnston 148; /Julie 88; /Dorling Kindersley 107 top left; /Fabrice Lerouge 16 bottom left, 23, 99; /Alex Mares-Manton 36, 63, 126; /Medioimages 113; /Tom Merton 151 bottom left; /Laurence Monneret 7 bottom right; /Andrew O'Toole 35 top right; /Jessica Peterson 15 top right; /Jose Luis Pelaez 151 top right; /PhotoAlto/Alix Minde 12; /PhotoAlto/Laurence Mouton 35 bottom left; /PhotoAlto/Odilon Dimier 151 top left, 161; /PhotoAlto/Sandro Di Carlo Darsa 154 bottom left; /Pink Fridge Productions 46-47; /Purestock 52, 118-119; /Stephanie Rausser 91 bottom right; /Gabrielle Revere 7 top left; /STasker 15 bottom left; /Stockbyte 135; /Thinkstock Images 77 top right; /Anne-Marie Weber 16 top left; /Jilly Wendell 154 bottom right; /Rachel Weill 15 bottom right; /Larry Williams 154 top right; /ZenShui/Laurence Mouton 11. **Masterfile** 39 bottom right, 72, 73, 96 bottom left, 120, 138-139; /Kevin Dodge 26; /Jon Feingersh 49; /Glowimages 19 top left; /Steven Puetzer 31; /Mark Tomalty 132. **Photolibrary Group**/Banana Stock 48; /Maike Jessen 16 top right; /Jutta Klee 91 top left; /Monkey Business Images Ltd. 78; /Sigrid Olsson 19 bottom left; /Stockbroker 91 top right.